THE
N°MAD

The Diaries of
Isabelle Eberhardt

Translated by Nina de Voogd
Introduction by Annette Kobak
Edited by Elizabeth Kershaw

I

Interlink Books
An imprint of Interlink Publishing Group, Inc.
Northampton

This edition first published in 2024 by

INTERLINK BOOKS
An imprint of Interlink Publishing Group, Inc.
46 Crosby Street
Northampton, Massachusetts 01060
www.interlinkbooks.com

Original English translation copyright © Nina de Voogd 1987, 2003, 2024
Edited translation first published by Virago Press in 1987

Published in Great Britain by Summersdale Publishers Ltd.
Additional translated text reproduced by permission of Annette Kobak,
    copyright © Annette Kobak 1988, 2003, 2012, 2024
Editor's notes copyright © Elizabeth Kershaw 2003, 2012, 2024
Introduction copyright © Annette Kobak 2003, 2012, 2024

Library of Congress Cataloging-in-Publication Data
Eberhardt, Isabelle, 1877–1904.
[Bonne nomade. English]
The nomad : the diaries of Isabelle Eberhardt / translated by Nina de Voogd ;
    edited by Elizabeth Kershaw ; introduction by Annette Kobak.—1st American ed.
    208 p. : map ; 21 cm.
Previously published: The passionate nomad. Boston : Beacon Press, 1988. (Virago/
    Beacon travelers). With new introd. Includes bibliographical references.
LCCN 2003004363 | ISBN 978-1-62371-710-0
1. Eberhardt, Isabelle, 1877–1904—Diaries. 2. Women—Algeria—Diaries.
    3. Algeria—Biography.
I. Kershaw, Liz. II. Eberhardt, Isabelle, 1877–1904. Diaries. English. Selections. III. Title.
DT294.7.E2A3 2003 | 961.03'092—dc21
LC record available at https://lccn.loc.gov/2003004363

9 8 7 6 5 4 3 2 1

Printed and bound in the United States of America

Annette Kobak's acclaimed biography *Isabelle: The Life of Isabelle Eberhardt* is
published by Virago Press, and she has translated Eberhardt's novel, *Vagabond*
(The Hogarth Press). Annette Kobak reviews regularly for *The New York Times
Book Review* and *The Times Literary Supplement*.

CONTENTS

Paris •

FRANCE

SWITZERLAND

Geneva •

ITALY

CORSICA

SPAIN

SARDINIA

Cagliari •

MEDITERRANEAN
SEA

Bône •

Tunis •

Monastir •

Algiers •

Constantine •

Tenès •

Batna •

ALGERIA

Biskra •

TUNISIA

Touggourt •

• El Oued

Aïn Sefra •

• Ouargla

INTRODUCTION

There can surely be no more striking opening to a diary than Isabelle Eberhardt's:

Cagliari, 1 January 1900
I am alone, sitting facing the grey expanse of the shifting sea . . . I am alone . . . alone as I've always been everywhere, as I'll always be throughout this seductive and deceptive universe . . .

From the island of Sardinia on the first day of a new century, Isabelle looks out onto a sombre, inscrutable sea as if it were the century ahead. She is only twenty-two, and she has less than five more years to live until her watery, extraordinary death, drowned in the desert. Although Isabelle had probably written a diary before this one, it has not survived, and there is no doubt she chose this sonorous date with care to begin what now stands as her first journal out of four. The originals themselves have been lost, and we know only from their first editor, René Louis Doyon, who published them in French in 1923, that they consisted of four notebooks, all – like most of her writings and papers – retrieved from the flash flood at Aïn Sefra in the Algerian Atlas mountains which killed her. Together, the diaries span three of the most dramatic years of her life until a year before her death on 21 October 1904.

The choice of date to begin is a measure of how considered her diaries were, in spite of their apparent nonchalance. They were not just the jottings of a wanderer keen to note down what she saw in a part of the world which other Europeans had rarely seen with such intimacy – though they were that too. ('While travelling,' she writes, 'I must carefully write down not only *factual information*, but also my *impressions*.') Isabelle was also trying to map herself day by day in order to discern a pattern which might serve as some anchorage to what she experienced as an unusually fragmented personality. From the first entry, the disparate selves come into play: the lone self, the dreamer, the 'real' self, as opposed to the mask of 'cynic, dissipated and debauched layabout' which she presents to outsiders. Contradictory selves are there even in the language, as Isabelle describes herself in the masculine – '*débauché*' and '*seul*' – although she is a young woman. And at the end of the entry she signs herself not Isabelle Eberhardt, but Mahmoud Essadi, her chosen Arab name. Even in her diary, the repository of her authentic self which she feels at this stage she has to hide from the world, several selves come into play – draft selves, as it were.

What Isabelle's diaries chart above all are the outer and inner journeys which forged those selves into a coherent identity. We follow her unparalleled solo journeyings across the breadth of Algeria, from Bône (now Annaba) to Constantine, Algiers, Tlemcen, Bou Saada, and El Oued (as well as episodes in Marseilles and Geneva), but we also follow her inner journey – the 'stages of her *via dolorosa*' as she puts it at a particularly bleak patch in her life – from dark despondency to 'a fruitful, salutary melancholia' and measure of inner peace – all this before the age of twenty-seven.

For the moment, though, from her temporary perch on the island of Sardinia and at the start of a new century, Isabelle is consciously poised between the Geneva of her troubled past and the North Africa of her Muslim future. The coincidence of the new century arriving just as she is sloughing off what she calls 'the debris of a lost past which has just collapsed in ruins' is too notable for her not to register. The life she left behind in her native city of Geneva was riddled with threatening mysteries and, above all, with losses. Within the last three years, her mother died suddenly in Bône, just as she and Isabelle had come over from their gloomy villa in Meyrin on the outskirts of Geneva as advance guard to try to set up a new life for their fraught household. The following year, in 1898, Vladimir, the only one of Isabelle's half brothers still left at home in Geneva, committed suicide by putting his head in a gas oven. A year later, the last remaining inhabitant of the villa, Alexander Trophimowsky, known as 'Vava', tutor to the family and unacknowledged father to Isabelle, died of throat cancer, nursed in his dying months by Isabelle. And three months later, in August 1899, Isabelle's only remaining family tie, her brother Augustin, married someone with whom Isabelle had no rapport, and she knew she had lost him to a dismal life as surely as she had done when he absconded years before to join the French Foreign Legion. Isabelle had much cause for grief. Her tone in the opening diary is steeped in shock at these deaths and losses, which she hadn't had time to mourn, and at the fact that she was now left alone in the world.

Yet the weight of melancholy which haunts the diary, the 'sad enigma of my own soul' or 'my unnameable sorrow' as she calls it later, has its roots even further in her past. Isabelle was born into secretive circumstances which weighed heavily on her without her knowing why. It is telling that Isabelle's neighbours in Meyrin remember glimpsing her in the sprawling garden always 'carrying things which were too heavy for her'. As she writes on 18 January 1900, 'I am, if you like, the scapegoat of all the sins and misfortunes which precipitated three people to their doom: Mother, Vladimir and Vava.'

For Isabelle was born into a situation which was, as it were, mined. At the age of nineteen her mother, *née* Nathalie Eberhardt, had married a sixty-three-year-old widower, General Pavel de Moerder, who held important positions in the Tsar's entourage both as military commander and, latterly, overseeing the Imperial police. Nathalie inherited two stepdaughters and a stepson, then produced two sons and a daughter of her own before leaving Russia for Switzerland on a voyage of convalescence. She took her stepson and her own children with her as well as their tutor Trophimowsky, the farouche Armenian-born former priest who had left behind a family of his own in Kherson on the Black Sea.

Trophimowsky was an anarchist, a curious choice as tutor for someone so close to the Tsar, even though his anarchism tended towards the self-sufficient, Tolstoyan kind. Soon after arriving in Geneva, Madame de Moerder gave birth to another son, Augustin, but after four months the news came through from Russia that the general had died of a heart attack. Madame de Moerder decided to stay in Switzerland and could still been seen as observing the proprieties until the moment four years later when, on 17 February 1877 and apparently out of the blue, she gave birth to Isabelle. Unable to admit the tutor's paternity to either the family in Russia or her older children, she registered Isabelle simply as her 'illegitimate daughter', without citing a father, and giving Isabelle her own maiden name.

As they grew up, the General's older children all sought to escape from the Villa, swearing vengeance on the disliked tutor who had abducted – as they saw it – their mother. To make matters worse, the eldest of Madame de Moerder's sons, Nicolas, joined the Ministry of Foreign Affairs under the autocratic Tsar Alexander III. From this influential position, he began to harass Trophimowsky, whom he accused of being his mother's lover and having murdered his father. In spite of all these accusations, which Isabelle was aware of at least from the age of eleven, Trophimowsky and Madame de Moerder never admitted to her that the man she knew as 'Vava' (shadowing 'Papa' so closely) was her father.

Although most of this is out of the frame of Isabelle's diaries, it rumbles in the background as distant thunder to their emotional and narrative content. No wonder she was determined to get away from the shadows of the past and lose herself in her adoptive country of Algeria, and particularly in the desert spaces of the Sahara. No wonder, too, that seeing the future century as a blank canvas on which she could rewrite herself had its appeal.

Isabelle had been to North Africa twice by the time the new century opened; once with her mother in 1897, and again on her own in the summer of 1899 after Trophimowsky's death. On this trip, starting from Tunis and travelling down to the beautiful southerly Algerian oasis of El Oued with whatever transport came her way – with *moyens de fortune* – she lived out for the first time her long-held dream of travelling alone in the Sahara. Dressing as a young Tunisian scholar, and picking up spoken Arabic along the way with her Slav facility for languages – and aided by the classical Arabic Trophimowsky had taught her at home – she steeped herself naturally in the everyday life of the villages, the *caravanes* and El Oued. 'Everyday life' in French is *'le journalier'*, which as a noun also means a 'day-labourer'. Isabelle – who briefly worked as a labourer on the docks in Marseilles (as the diaries record) and who had been trained by Trophimowsky to take a philosophic pride in labouring in the garden at the Villa in the afternoons, whilst studying in the mornings – chose the name '*Mes Journaliers*' for her diaries. It was a nice coining of a new word for 'journals', with added layers of meaning. Trophimowsky's egalitarian anarchism led him to dress his female charges as boys throughout their childhood, so that dressing and acting as a young Muslim man came easily to Isabelle.

But for Isabelle – unlike, say, Richard Burton on his journey to Mecca – her dress was not so much a disguise as a reclothing of herself in her rightful mind, a becoming of the person she was underneath – the 'real me'. It also, of course, enabled her to travel freely in a way she could never have done dressed as a European or Arab woman at the end of the nineteenth century. There was a long-standing tradition of female *maraboutes*, Islamic saints and mystics, in Algeria, so for her to pose as an itinerant Koranic scholar would not have been seen as strange by the local Algerians, even if they knew at once that she was a woman, as many did.

Isabelle returned definitively to El Oued and Algeria from autumn 1900, but although she was free of the entanglements of her former life, she would not be living in the carefree way she had in the summer of 1899. This was partly because she was now virtually without financial resources, as the sale of the Villa had been disastrously mismanaged, and also because she had met a young Algerian soldier, Slimène Ehnni, who would become her husband. Although it was an unconventional marriage as she retained most of her independent ways, it rooted her more firmly in the ordinary life of Algeria – *le journalier* – and particularly in the indigenous life as it was affected, and often oppressed, by

the colonial government of the French. Although she finally
became close to the French marshal, Lyautey, who prepared
the way for the eventual takeover of Morocco on behalf of
the French, Isabelle's sympathies were always with the local
people, particularly with the *fellahs* – the peasants and the
poor. The Sufi fraternity which she joined, the Qadrya, was
not only the oldest of the Sufi sects, but the one which
involved itself most with help for the indigent.

If Isabelle had hoped to find spiritual peace in the Sahara,
and she did, it became vitiated by a life as dangerously
eventful as before. There would even be as much cloak-and-
dagger as – literally so: a fellow Sufi made an attempt on her
life with a sabre, narrowly missing killing her. Inwardly, and
without melodrama, she took this as a sign of what she had
always sensed: that she was in some way predestined for
some unusual fate, perhaps to be a mystic. She calls it 'the
maraboutic question' in the diaries, wondering whether 'all
this isn't the direct path to religious mysticism!' In fact the
assassination attempt turned out to be a turning-point in her
life, reconciling her to her strange destiny, and in a sense
making her take responsibility for it. Her pardoning of her
would-be assassin Abdallah Mohammed ben Lakhdar and
successful bid to mitigate his life sentence were acts of
impressive inner maturity. The letters she wrote about this
episode to the local newspapers – included here – show her
great lucidity, intelligence and tact.

This contact with the newspapers, and Mohammed's trial,
put her in the public eye for the first time. Tales of 'the good
nomad' and the 'Amazon of the Sahara' began to reach a Paris
eager for such spicy fare. From now on Isabelle would live a
more publicly accountable life, although always subordinate
to her inner quest for peace and 'spiritual progress' and to
her cherished solitary journeys into the *souf* or Sahara.

Outside the framework of the extant diaries, in the last year and three quarters of her life, Isabelle and Slimène moved to the northern coastal towns of Ténès and Algiers, where Isabelle began to work for Victor Barrucand, the editor of the French–Arabic newspaper *L'Akhbar*, reporting skirmishes on the borders of Morocco and Algeria. Following the army and caravans of the local tribes, she sent back regular dispatches under the title *Sud-Oranais*. She also became a close friend and colleague of General Lyautey, and spent some time in a Moroccan monastery at his behest. She found a new, luminous and subtle peace there, before going to Lyautey's barracks town of Aïn Sefra, deep in the southern Atlas mountains, to be treated for fever. It is here that she was suddenly overwhelmed by the thunderous flash flood that killed her and twenty-three others. Slimène managed to escape.

Isabelle left behind over two thousand pages of notes, articles and fiction. Apart from the diaries, there were four posthumous volumes of stories about desert, village and town life in the Maghreb, much of it affected by the clash of codes between the occupying colonial forces and the local inhabitants, but also full of evocative descriptions of natural beauty. In addition she left two novels, *Le Trimardeur* and *Rakhil* (unfinished). For someone called 'too lazy to live' by one of her biographers, she had not done too badly. (Some of her favourite writers she mentions in the journals, Baudelaire, Edmond Goncourt, Loti and Tolstoy had published nothing by the age of twenty-seven.)

Most of all, though, she gave a voice to those who were ordinarily occluded from literature or history: the dispossessed (as she always felt herself to be in spirit), the poor, those caught between cultures. She did this against the grain of her times, when it was not fashionable to espouse Algeria's cause. Although Orientalism was in vogue, and French writers like André Gide, Gustave Flaubert and Pierre Loti had been to North Africa and written about it, Isabelle was not an 'Orientalist' as they were. She was not even a travel writer in the conventional Western sense: she stayed in the country, she steeped herself in its life. This is reflected even in her writing, which marries French, Arabic, Russian and Latin words in the same open spirit that she took to the open road: a kind of literary vagabondage, a natural integration. Her stories now stand as an invaluable cornerstone of a new, post-colonial Maghrebian literature, recording a way of life which was vanishing under the pressures of the modern world.

Isabelle was also a European, however, and is as aware of the impact of Arab life on a European sensibility as she is of that of the coloniser on the native Algerian. She was the first woman (to my knowledge) to have written of the seductively annihilating effect of the southern regions, as André Gide did in *L'Immoraliste* and Paul Bowles (a fan of Isabelle's writing) did in *The Sheltering Sky*. In his book *In Patagonia*, Bruce Chatwin puts words to the phenomenon when he writes, 'Poe, like Coleridge whom he idolised, is another night-wandering man, obsessed by the Far South and by voyages of annihilation and rebirth.' Carl Jung saw the effect too, in North Africa and, in his *Memories, Dreams, Reflections*, linked it to travelling back into the collective unconscious: 'The deeper we penetrated into the Sahara, the more time slowed down for me; it even threatened to move backwards.' It is a sentiment Isabelle foreshadows in her diary: 'The impression was a biblical one, and I suddenly felt as if transported back to the ancient days of primitive humanity, when the great light-giving bodies in the sky had been the object of veneration.'

There is a paradox here. Isabelle, far ahead of her times in claiming a fierce independence of action and of thought as a young woman, was also travelling backwards in time, into a more ancient, submissive and vibrant culture. Indeed, this is the central journey and motif of her life: the journey from north to south, from Europe to the Maghreb (the indigenous name she always uses for North Africa), from the fin-de-siècle nihilism and anarchism she was born into to Islam. Its pattern is repeated in the lives of many of the characters in her short stories and fiction. Islam appealed to her from early on as a solution to the wrong turnings she felt the Western world was taking in its attitudes to colonising other cultures and to the spiritual and physical life. The figure of the *taleb*, the staunchly anti-colonialist divinity student, appears in one of her earliest pieces, 'Visions of the Maghreb', published in Paris before she had even been to North Africa. Isabelle in effect became that *taleb* when she slipped into the mantle of Si Mahmoud Essadi on her first visit to Tunisia.

Trophimowsky had sown the seeds of her interest in Islam with his teachings, but Isabelle was probably introduced to a more purist, militant version of Islam through one of her earliest Islamic contacts, Ali Abdul Wahab, a Tunisian friend of her brother Augustin's. From a long correspondence with the scholarly Wahab before she even set foot in North Africa, Isabelle was introduced to a reformist strain of Islam known as Wahabism (sometimes Wahhabism) deriving from Ali's own family dynasty. Wahabism had for centuries challenged Islam to return to the severe simplicity of its Koranic roots – and still does. (The Wahabi family also married into the

Saudi dynasty and were co-founders of Saudi Arabia.) Many of the original followers of Wahabism were Bedouins, but the sect also advocated things with which we have become all too familiar recently, namely the putting to death of all unbelievers, and the immediate entrance into Paradise for soldiers who fell in battle. And there is no denying the militancy of Isabelle's own initial passion for Islam: in March 1899, when she was in Tunisia in her persona as a *taleb* shortly after her mother's death, she took part in violent fighting in Bône on the side of the Muslims who were protesting against colonial rule and alleged Christian insults to Islam. She writes in her notebook, 'perhaps I shall be fighting for the Muslim revolutionaries like I used to for the Russian anarchists . . . although with more conviction and with more real *hatred* against oppression. I feel now that I'm much more deeply a Muslim than I was an anarchist.' And in her diaries she writes of her 'heart both proud and unswerving in its commitment to Islam, a cause for which I long some day to spill the hot blood that courses through my veins,' and – categorically – 'Whoever considers themselves to be a Muslim must devote themselves body and soul to Islam for all time, to the point of martyrdom if need be; Islam must inhabit their soul, and govern every one of their acts and words.' *Taleb*, of course, shares a root with Taliban, and in these early encounters the *taleb* Isabelle's Islamic fervour verges on fanaticism.

Isabelle's allegiance to Islam shows through in the fabric of her life in different ways at different stages – though always in some oblique way as a counterpoise to her melancholy. She states in her letter to *Dépêche Algérienne* of 7 June 1901 (reproduced in the diaries) that she had been a

Muslim 'for a very long time', and even claimed a Muslim
father at one point in one of the many obfuscations over her
birth – although it is possible that Trophimowsky's
knowledge of Islam qualified him for that role, at least in
Isabelle's subconscious. Symbolically, though, Isabelle
became a Muslim on that first journey with her mother to
Bône in 1897. For both women, the journey was the
equivalent of a *hejra*, in Islamic tradition a radical departure
from the beliefs of the past and a total submission to the
new faith – Islam, which itself in Arabic means submission
to God. There is even an echo perhaps of that moment in
Isabelle's opening diary entry, as she lets go of the past and
looks out to a new future from such a watershed date.

And yet the reality of her life was far from being single-
mindedly Islamic, as her writer friend Robert Randau teased
her – and as she had to agree. In her own words, Islam may
have inhabited her soul, but it didn't govern every one of
her acts and words. After all, she smoked *kef*, she drank
alcohol, she led a determinedly free sexual life, and she
wandered at will on foot, horseback or caravan in a way she
could never have done if she had become what a strict
Islamic code would have decreed: a Muslim woman, in
woman's dress. She was only able to espouse Islam and still
be her complex self by dressing as a man. After her marriage
to Slimène, himself caught between two cultures as an *évolué*
– a Gallicized Algerian – and after her increasing involvement
with Barrucand and Lyautey, Isabelle began instinctively to
accommodate and integrate Western and Islamic influences
just as she had naturally done with her writing. She noted
towards the end of her life, 'Inevitably, in many ways we
wronged the native people, who did not ask us to come . . .
we make amends to some extent by more intense
cultivation, but we shall only really be at peace with

ourselves the day when sympathy replaces antipathy.' Isabelle Eberhardt/Si Mahmoud Essadi had already led the way by making this journey within herself. Perhaps even her journey into the past, into Islam, was ironically enough as ahead of her time as the rest of her; picking up on the fault line between Islam and the West which would rumble through into our own new century and once again become contemporary.

Certainly, through her courageously forged life, she was on her way to marrying the warring selves she had at first found so hard to reconcile. It was her tragedy that she didn't live long enough to see this through to a more rewarding fulfilment. But then her many selves served her writing well, and she was above all a writer, not a polemicist: as she had written to Ali Abdul Wahab as early as 1898, 'Literature is my polar star.'

Annette Kobak

EDITOR'S FOREWORD

Isabelle Eberhardt is a fascinating subject: elusive, frustrating, multiple, awkward; at once an editor's dream and nightmare. A vivid character, yet comprised of shadows, each of which purports to be the 'true' Isabelle, and each of which in a way is, as much as the next.

In her book *Isabelle*, Annette Kobak, to whose knowledge and assistance I am indebted, has written of the biographer's fear; that of just missing the point, of getting it slightly but vitally wrong. This is particularly pertinent in an attempt to do justice to Isabelle Eberhardt's life, and of editing the written work most intimate to her: her diaries. Inevitably, this volume is not an unabbreviated record. Although at times she reread and rewrote her notes, in writing her diary Isabelle was not composing for a reader and wrote with an erratic selectivity. I have left alone Isabelle's changeability and contradictions, though I have found it wise to exclude material that seemed largely irrelevant (lists of times of arrival; jottings of complete sections of quoted material, largely from Pierre Loti; repetitious entries). In attempting to provide a framework to her words and filling in some of the ellipses, I have tried to maintain a neutral tone so as not to interfere with Isabelle's voice.

Isabelle's diaries comprised three cardboard notebooks and a small linen volume whose cover was faded by mud during the flood that cost her her life. She used her diaries for observation and introspection; to record literary ideas; as a ledger and as a portable library of copied material from her favourite writers. She wrote principally in French, using both masculine and feminine forms when referring to herself, and was an accomplished linguist, able to speak and write Latin, Greek, Italian and German, and was also fluent in Arabic and Russian, using both in her diary. To clarify a change of language in this translation, passages in Arabic are preceded by a crescent ∪, and those in Russian by a cross +. Isabelle used a number of names in reference to her close family: the White Spirit and the 'white dove' were terms for her mother; Vava for Trophimowsky, her mother's lover and the man believed to be her father; Ouïha, Rouh' and Zouïzou, meaning 'beloved' in Arabic, were endearments for her lover, later her husband, Slimène Ehnni.

Isabelle's story does not end at her death. As late as the 1950s Cecily Mackworth remarked on researching her book, *The Destiny of Isabelle Eberhardt*, that Isabelle was still very much a contentious figure in France and North Africa; acknowledged as a writer but frowned upon as a champion of licentiousness, the debauchee of the desert. In the 1960s Isabelle became a cult figure for the freedom generation, revered for precisely those things that had caused her to be so despised. However, it is perhaps now that Isabelle and her story seem most contemporary. Caught between cultures, between races; torn between old teachings and new ideas; embroiled in the clash of misunderstandings between East and West; shifting between identities, guises and ambitions, Isabelle's is a profoundly modern parable – and an applicable history.

Isabelle could not avoid being political, but neither could she depersonalise, and the deeper I have delved into her life, the more I am struck by her individuality, her capacity to confound and surprise. Do I, though, know the *real* Isabelle any better after all this research? Perhaps tellingly not, but I remain intrigued, lastingly impressed by this incredible woman.

Elizabeth Kershaw

THE NOMAD

diaries of Isabelle Eberhardt

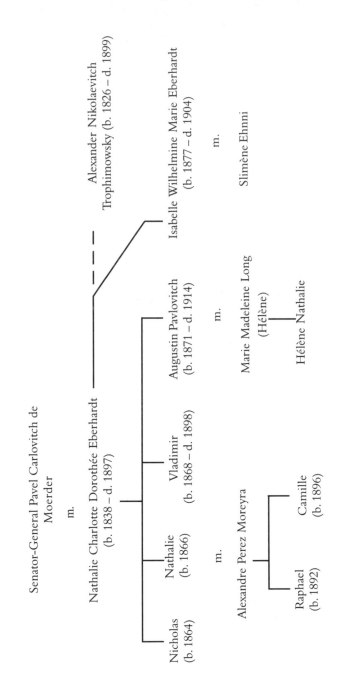

Senator-General Pavel Carlovitch de Moerder

m.

Nathalie Charlotte Dorothée Eberhardt (b. 1838 – d. 1897)

Alexander Nikolaevitch Trophimowsky (b. 1826 – d. 1899)

Isabelle Wilhelmine Marie Eberhardt (b. 1877 – d. 1904)

m.

Slimène Ehnni

Nicholas (b. 1864)

Nathalie (b. 1866)

m.

Alexandre Perez Moreyra

Raphael (b. 1892)

Camille (b. 1896)

Vladimir (b. 1868 – d. 1898)

Augustin Pavlovitch (b. 1871 – d. 1914)

m.

Marie Madeleine Long (Hélène)

Hélène Nathalie

JOURNAL ONE

Isabelle Eberhardt's diary begins after a mournful period in her life, which in succession sees the death of her beloved mother in an earlier visit to North Africa in 1897, the suicide of her elder brother Vladimir in 1898 and the fatal illness of the man suspected to be her father, Alexander Trophimowsky, in 1899. Used to increased freedom found in her youth when dressed as a boy, Isabelle has been journeying in Africa as her male alter-ego, Mahmoud Essadi (or Si Mahmoud), a young Tunisian scholar. She returns only periodically to France. Her explorations have been both sexual as well as geographical. The start of a new century sees Isabelle's arrival in Sardinia.

Cagliari, 1 January 1900
I am alone, sitting facing the grey expanse of the shifting sea . . . I am alone . . . alone as I've always been everywhere, as I'll always be throughout this seductive and deceptive universe . . . alone, with a whole world of dashed hopes, disappointment and disillusion behind me, and of memories that grow daily more distant, almost losing all reality.

My soul is tempered now for good, and now is indestructible, resolute even through the worst storms, devastations or loss. My knowledge of life and the human heart is now so keen that I know the two months ahead will bring me more sorrow, largely because I will not pander to mundanities nor to anything alien to the dreams, thoughts and feelings of my true personality.

Seen from the outside, I wear the mask of the cynic, the dissipated and debauched layabout. No one yet has managed to see through to my real inner self, which is sensitive and pure and which rises above the humiliation and baseness I choose to wallow in. No one has ever understood that even though I may seem to be driven by the senses alone, my heart is in fact generous, one that used to overflow with love and tenderness and continues to be filled with boundless compassion for all those who suffer injustice, all those who are weak and oppressed . . . a heart both proud and unswerving in its commitment to Islam, a cause for which I long some day to spill the hot blood that courses through my veins. I shall dig in my heels, therefore, and go on acting the drunken, plate-smashing degenerate, steeping her wild, besotted mind in the intoxicating expanse of desert as I did last summer, or galloping through olive groves in the Tunisian Sahel, as I did in the autumn.

Who will ever treat me to those silent nights again, those lazy rides on horseback through the salty plains of the Oued Righ's and the Oued Souf's white sands? Who will recreate the feeling, at once sad and blissful, that would fill my pariah's heart every time I struck some sort of chaotic camp surrounded by friends made on the spot among Spahis and nomads, none of whom ever took me for the despicable outcast I had become so miserably at the hands of fate? Who will send me on those wild rides again through the Sahel's plains and valleys while the autumn wind blows, rides so intoxicating and sublime I used to lose all notion of reality!

Right now I long for only one thing: to reclothe myself in that cherished personality, the real and true one, and to go back to Africa again. I long to sleep in the cool, deep silence, beneath the dizzying volley of stars, with nothing but the sky's infinite expanse for a roof and the warm earth for a bed . . . to doze off in the sorrowful yet serene knowledge that I am utterly alone, that no one pines for me *anywhere on earth*, that there is no place where I am being missed or expected. To know all that, to be free and without ties, a nomad camped in life's great desert, where I shall never be anything but an outsider, a stranger and an intruder. Such is the only form of bliss, however bitter, the *Mektoub* will ever grant me. Happiness of the sort coveted by all of frantic humanity, will never be mine.

Why still bother with illusions? The light went out of my life when, two years ago, my white dove lay down to sleep in Bône's Cimetière des Croyants.[1]

Now that Vava[2] has returned to dust as well, and nothing is left of all that once seemed so solid and so permanent, now that all is gone, vanished, for all time and eternity! . . . and now that fate has so curiously, so mysteriously driven a wedge between myself and the only being who ever came close enough to my true nature to catch however pale a glimpse of it, Augustin . . .[3]

And now that . . . Enough! I must put all those recent events to rest once and for all.

From now on, I shall drift along on life's random waves . . . I shall turn to every possible wellspring for intoxication, without a thought for the fact that they are all doomed to run dry in the end . . . No more of those struggles, victories and defeats that have always left me bleeding from a wounded heart . . . No more adolescent follies!

I am here out of friendship for the man Fate put across my path[4] just as I was in the midst of a crisis – ∪ *please Allah*, may it be the last one, although my feeling of friendship is all the stronger for it.

I realise that once again I am about to steep myself in the *ineffable*, in the realm of things I feel and understand so clearly but have never managed to express.

Yet never will I curse this pitiful life of mine nor even this wretched universe . . . where love goes hand in hand with death, and all is fleeting and impermanent. They have both given me raptures too profound for that, ecstasies too sweet, too many dreams and thoughts. I no longer regret or long for anything . . . all I do is *wait*.

As a nomad who has no fatherland besides Islam and neither family nor close friends, who is alone, eternally alone in the quiet solitude of her sombre soul, I shall wend my way through life until it will be time for that great everlasting sleep inside the grave . . .

MAHMOUD ESSADI

The perennial, mysterious and frightening question remains; where will I be, on which soil and underneath which sky, at this time a year from now? Far away no doubt from this small Sardinian town . . . Where though? And will I still be alive?

Cagliari, 7 January 1900
Impressions in a park, around 5 p.m.
A savage landscape, the jagged outlines of deeply gutted hills of either a red or grey colour; cavalcades of maritime pines and Barbary fig trees. Greenery so lush

it is almost out of place in the heart of winter. Salt lagoons with surfaces the colour of lead, dead and immobile like desert shotts. And up there at the very top, the town's silhouette straddles the steep and furrowed hillside. Ancient ramparts and a square, old, crenellated tower, levels of geometrically shaped roofs, all of it cast in pink, standing out against an indigo sky.

Near the very top, more greenery, and barracks identical to the ones in Algeria, long and low buildings with red-tiled roofs and flaky, peeling walls. Walls distempered to have the flaming pink, blood-red or sky-blue colours of Arab houses. Dark, old churches full of marble statues and mosaics, objects of sheer luxury in a country where poverty is the rule. Vaulted passageways make for resounding footsteps and booming echoes. A maze of alleyways going up and down, and intersected here and there by steps of grey stone; and because there is no traffic in a town located at this height, the tiny, pointed paving stones are all covered with spindly yellowish-green grass.

Doors lead to vast cellars below street level where whole poverty-stricken families live in age-old dankness. Other entrances afford glimpses of vaulted hallways and tiled stairwells.

Shops with small, loud-coloured window displays; Oriental boutiques, narrow and full of smoke where one can hear the drawl of nasal voices . . . Here and there a young man leans against a wall and makes signs to a girl bending over the railing of her balcony . . . Peasants wearing headdresses that hang all the way down their backs and black jackets pleated over their white calico trousers. Tanned and bearded men with deep-set eyes, heavy eyebrows and fierce, wary faces; a strange mixture of Greek mountain dwellers and Kabyles.[5]

There is an Arab beauty about the women. The expression in their language and melancholy, large, jet-black eyes is resigned and sad like that of wary animals.

Beggars whine obsequiously in their incessant pursuit of the stranger everywhere he goes . . . Songs that sound infinitely sad, refrains turn into a curiously gripping obsession, cantilenas just like those heard in Africa, a place one cannot help but feverishly long for here.

Isabelle records her impressions and memories of the Villa Neuve, her childhood home. The house is to be sold following the deaths of her mother and Trophimowsky, but legal wrangles with the elder children, clear and legitimate de Moerder issue, prevent any transaction or inheritance, a problem that is to have dire effect upon Isabelle's welfare.

Cagliari, Thursday 18 January, 5:30 in the afternoon
From my arrival here, memories of *La Villa Neuve* haunt me more and more . . . good and bad alike. I say good as well, because I must not be unfair to the poor old place now that it's all dead and gone. I must not forget that it sheltered Mother and her gentle kindness, Vava and all his good intentions, which were never realised and, above all, my chaotic dreams.

No, heaping curses on those old days will not do, in spite of my lack of freedom there. Since I finally left that house, my life has been nothing but a swift and dream-like flash, moving through various lands, under different names and guises.

I realise that the fairly restful winter I am spending here is but a breathing spell from the kind of life that will be mine until the very end. In a few days' time, my true way of life and its aimless wanderings will take over again. Where? How? Only God can tell. I must not even dare speculate any longer: just as I was about to decide to stay on in Paris for months on end, I ended up in out-of-the-way Cagliari of all places. So no more guesswork or conjecture.

Yet one thing delights me: the farther I get from the limbo of the past, the more my character is strengthening in just the way I wanted it to. What is developing in me is the most stubborn and unconquerable energy, and an integrity of spirit, two qualities that I value more than any other and which are, alas, so very rare in a woman.

The likely prospect of spending four months in the desert next spring makes me feel confident of making a name for myself, of becoming somebody, and, through that alone, of achieving my life's goal: revenge! Vava is dead, Augustin is once and for all headed for life's beaten tracks . . . The only one left is I myself.[6]

Fortunately, everything about my past life and adolescence have taught that peaceful happiness is not made for me, and that, alone amongst men, I am destined for a relentless struggle against them, that I am, if you like, the scapegoat for all the sins and misfortunes which precipitated three people to their doom: Mother, Vladimir and Vava.

I am now about to play my part. I enjoy it more than I would any selfish pleasure, and plan to give up all I hold dear for it. That is a goal I shall pursue for the rest of my life.

I have given up the hope of ever having a corner on earth to call my own, a home, a family, peace and prosperity. I have donned the cloak of the rootless wanderer, one that can be a burden too at times. I have written off the thought of ever coming home to a happy family for rest and safety.

For the moment I have found a soothing enough temporary home here in Cagliari, and have the illusion of truly loving someone whose presence seems to have become a must[7]. . . that dream will be short-lived. I shall need to be alone again, away from the tranquil indolence of a shared existence and on the rough and risky road of travel.

That is what must be, and so it shall be. And in the gloom of that future existence I shall at least have one consolation, the thought that upon my return a friend, a living being, may be delighted to see me again. What is so terrible though, is the length of time spent apart to make for such reunions . . . And who knows, someone else may have taken my place by then. That is more than likely, given his ideas about women and marriage. It would be very strange indeed if he were never to meet a woman with whom to share those ideas, which are so at odds with mine. I know that no such partner will appear while he is a vagabond outcast, unless he is prepared to make do with a wife somewhere who will quiver at the mere thought of him in danger – but only from a safe and comfortable distance. A woman like myself, though, the kind who will brave any obstacle to be at his side in times of need, he will not find.

But then he too, like Augustin and everybody else, will yield to the lure of home and comfort once the present period of transition is behind him.

When that happens I will have no choice but to resume my journey, sad but certain of having nothing to look forward to but the empty hotel rooms, *gourbis* and tents that are the nomad's temporary shelter. ∪ *Mektoub!*[8] The only thing to do is to take things as they come and enjoy this heady interlude, for it will soon be over.

~~~~~~~~~~~

'Why do human lives not end like the African Autumn, in a clear sky, tepid winds and neither decrepitude nor forebodings of any sort?'
 Une Année dans le Sahel, Eugène Fromentin

Written at Cagliari
In a moment of bottomless sadness brought on by nothing in particular.

~~~~~~~~~~~

Cagliari, 29 January 1900
The brief interlude in this ancient Sardinian town has now come to an end. Tomorrow at this time I shall be far from these Cagliari cliffs, on the leaden, grumbling, turbulent sea.

Last night, Cagliari was booming with the echo of the sea's rolling thunder . . . Today, it was its most ominous; it had a dull and glaucous shimmer. This beloved hovel looks a desolate wreck in tonight's grey sunset, the very image of departure and upheaval, and I am full of the sorrow that goes with changes in surroundings, those successive stages of annihilation that slowly lead to the great and final void.

And what will be the next stage?

Isabelle returns to Geneva, staying for a while in Paris in order to further her literary career.

Geneva, Sunday 27 May 1900, 9:30 p.m.
Back to this gloomy diary of mine in this evil city in which I have suffered so much. I have hardly been here a week and once again I feel as morbid and oppressed as I used to in the old days. All I want to do is get out for good.

I went to have a look at our poor house, with the sky low and sunless; the place was boarded up, mute and lost amongst the weeds. I saw the road, white as ever, white like a silvery river, straight as an arrow, heading between those tall, velvet trees for the Jura's great mountaintops.

I saw the two graves in that faithless cemetery,[9] set in a land of exile, so very far away from that sacred place devoted to eternal repose and everlasting silence . . .[10] I feel that I have now become a total stranger in this land, and tonight I feel an unfathomable and indescribable sadness, and increasingly resigned before my fate . . . What dreams, what enchantments and what raptures does the future still hold in store for me? What dubious satisfactions, and what sorrows?

And when will the clock strike the hour of deliverance at long last, the hour of eternal rest?

(Recorded later) Paris, April 1900
In the misty light of stars and street lamps one night, I saw the Montparnasse cemetery's white crosses outlined like so many ghosts against the velvety black of large trees, and it occurred to me that the powerful breath of Paris one can hear rumbling all around had no way of interfering with the everlasting slumber of all the strangers lying there . . .

JOURNAL TWO

Quickly tiring of Paris and developing a dislike for its fin de siècle artificialities and affectations, Isabelle returns to Geneva, principally to put her effects in order so that she can leave for North Africa at short notice.

In the name of God, the Merciful, the Compassionate!

~~~~~~~~~~

'Now no more grief and pain is owing to you
I know you die in this world to be born in the next.'

Epitaph in Italian found on a grave in the little Vernier cemetery on 4 June 1899, the day I left Geneva and made a last pilgrimage to Vava's grave.

Peace to your ashes, to those that lie buried
In that far-off foreign country, and to you who
Rest upon that sacred mound above the
Mediterranean's
Eternal blue waves . . .
  + *My hand is being directed by you who love me, and any false note would have tormented you in your sleep.*

~~~~~~~~~~

Geneva, 8 June 1900
Upon my return from the Vernier cemetery. Feeling infinitely sad.

The Nomad

'So much travelling will put the mind to sleep; one gets used to anything, whether to the most outstandingly exotic places or the most remarkable faces. Yet there are times when one suddenly wakes up and takes stock, only to be suddenly struck by the strangeness of one's surroundings.'
   Le Mariage de Loti, Pierre Loti

Over there in Africa, above the great blue gulf of unforgettable Annaba, the graveyard on the hill is asleep under the blazing sky of a summer day's sunset. The white marble tombs and those made of glazed and multicoloured tiles must look like bright flowers among the tall, black cypresses, creepers and geraniums the colour of blood or pale flesh, and fig trees from the Barbary Coast . . .

At that same moment, I was sitting in the low grass of another graveyard. As I sat facing the two grey tombs set among the spring weeds, I thought of that other grave, the + *White Spirit's* resting place . . . And in the midst of all that indestructible nature, my thoughts turned once again to the mystery of the end of people's lives.

Birds sang their innocent, peaceful song above the untold amount of human dust accumulated there . . .

So far, this diary can be summed up as follows: an endless record of the unfathomable sadness there is at the bottom of my life, it consists of increasingly vague allusions, not to people I have met or to facts that I have observed, but to the invariably melancholy effect these facts and people have upon me.

How useless and funereal are these notes of mine, and how despairingly monotonous, without even the slightest hint of lightness or of hope. The only consolation they contain is their increasing Islamic resignation.

At long last I do find that my soul is beginning to show signs of *indifference* to pedestrian things and people, which means that my strength is on the increase. I find it contemptible and unworthy of myself that for so long I have put so much store by pitiful things and by futile, meaningless encounters. At long last, the realisation that I am *utterly incapable of joining any coterie whatsoever, and of feeling at ease with people* whose only reason for being together is no mere happenstance but rather the fact that they share their lives.

For the time being at least I know what I want: I would like it if Archivir[11] understood the things I said and wrote to him. I would like him to smile at me as only he can, to hear him tell me in that tone of voice of his, the way he did the day I came so close to baring my soul: 'Go Mahmoud, and do great, magnificent deeds . . . Be a hero . . .'

It is true that of all the men I have come across, this one, whose beloved picture I have in front of me, is the most bewitching of all, and that his charm is of the most elevated and noble sort: he speaks to the spirit rather than to the senses, he exalts whatever is sublime and stifles the base and lowly. No one has ever had such a truly beneficial effect upon my soul. No one has ever understood and bolstered those blessed manifestations that, since the + *White Spirit's* death, have slowly but surely begun to take root in my heart: faith, repentance, the desire for moral perfection, the longing for a reputation based on noble *merit*, a sensuality that makes a mockery of my suffering and abnegation, a thirst for great and magnificent deeds. I judge and love him for what I have seen of him so far.

Time will tell whether I have been perceptive, whether I have seen him as he really is, or whether I have made another mistake. I will not swear to anything, but nothing has so far given me reason for suspicion, even though I have become terribly, incurably wary. If he is but another dissembler and a sham . . . that will be the end of it once and for all, for if what I hold to be pure turns out to have a hidden blemish, if what looks to me like true beauty masks the usual horror, if the light I take to be a beneficial star showing me the way or a beacon in life's black maze is but a trick meant to lead wayfarers astray – if so, what can I expect after that? Yet, once again, nothing, absolutely nothing has so far suggested there might be anything to such unthinkable conjecture . . . if he is the way I think he is, he may well put me through terrible but magnificent paces . . . he may well turn out to be responsible for sending me off to die, but spare me the worst of fates, namely disillusionment.

Geneva, 15 June 1900

Thus said the Lord, Stand ye in the ways, and see, and ask for the old paths, where is the good way, and walk therein, and ye shall find rest for your souls.
Jeremiah 6:16

I shall always cherish the memory of these past few days spent in greater *happiness* for they are moments stolen from life's hopelessness, so many hours snatched from the void.

I will only ever be drawn to people who suffer from that special and fertile anguish called self-doubt, or the thirst for the ideal, and desire for the soul's mystical fire. Self satisfaction because of some material accomplishment will never be for me: the truly great are those who quest for better spiritual selves. Not for me are those who feel smug, happy with themselves and their lot, content with the state of their heart and soul.

Not for me those solid citizens who are *deaf, dumb and blind and never admit to their wrongs.*

I must learn to *think.* That may be painful and take time, but without it there can be no such thing as individual happiness or inspiration and sense of worth.

I cannot describe the contempt and loathing I have for my own inadequacy, my obsessive need to see people, however banal, to prostitute my heart and soul and go into sickening explanations.

Instead of looking in myself for what my soul requires, why do I look in others, where I know it cannot be found?

Oh, why can't I get rid of all the superfluous rubbish and react against this impulse that continues to encumber my life? Except with people of a very rare sort, there is no such thing as communication on an intellectual plane, so why insist on courting disappointment?

LITERARY IDEAS

I think that, as a beginner, I must first of all develop the artistic side of my work, that is to say my *style*. *Rakhil*, as solely a plea in favour of the Koran and against the prejudices of the modern Muslim world, will interest no one.[12]

As a song of eternal love, beautiful in form, with melodious sentences and glittering images, *Rakhil* will intoxicate the heart of a sensualist, or anyone in love with art, which amounts to the same thing.

A striking symbol of what my life is now all about, and probably always will be, is that sign saying '*Room for rent*' over there, by the window of the seedy room I am living in, surrounded by a camp bed, papers and my handful of books.

How ironic and how sad. Nothing could express more clearly my deep solitude, my absolute abandonment in the middle of this vast universe.

Geneva, 16 June 1900, three o'clock in the afternoon
Following a night of suffering, a strange morning . . .
I realise that I cannot write right now.

I shall confine myself to describing the situation: a purely cerebral wish to improve my conduct and get to work . . . no enthusiasm, though, for either.

I am becoming aware of my growing resolve to set off for Ouargla at any cost, to try once more to isolate myself for months on end in the total silence of the desert and get used to that slow and dream-like life out there.[13]

Come to think of it, nothing is standing in my way. However limited my means, I will still be able to afford to live there as well as it is wise to live, and I have not forgotten all that I went through there, the unbelievable hardships, my illness . . . however, these must have been due to unfortunate circumstances, and the idea now appeals greatly. This time round, life in the desert will be less exhausting and it will complete my education as a man of action, the Spartan sort of education I need.

What bitter ecstasies await me: first the farewells over here, to that strange man Archivir, who has given me such a remarkable time, sweet and bitter all at once. Next, the solemn occasion of my boarding ship at Marseilles and saying goodbye to the brother who is the apple of my eye. Then the sad but soothing moment of my pilgrimage to Annaba, to her grave on that hallowed hillside.

Then to Batna, where I left behind so many nostalgic memories . . . Torrid Biskra, where I used to spend such charming evenings in front of the Moorish cafés . . . And that steep and blistering road to arid Oued Rir . . . And sad Touggourt sleeping beneath its shroud of salt, overlooking its hidden shott . . . And finally Ouargla, a place I have never seen, at the very gateway to the mysterious void: the great Sahara, which so draws my imagination . . .

Geneva, Wednesday 27 June 1900
I would like to go to Ouargla, settle there and *make a home, something I miss more and more.* A little house made of mud close to some date palms, a place to cultivate

the odd vegetable in the oasis, a servant and companion named Ahmed, a few animals to warm my lonely heart, a horse perhaps – a dream in other words, to be realised in time – and books as well.

To lead two lives; one that is full of adventure and belongs to the desert, and one, calm and restful, devoted to thought and far from all that might interfere with it.

I should also want to travel now and then, to visit Augustin, and go to Paris, and then return to my solitary, silent retreat. I must fashion a soul for myself out there, an awareness, an intelligence and a will. I have no doubt that the Islamic faith I need so much would blossom magnificently over there, and one day this notebook of mine may well take the place of a whole library, of all the books I will not have during my wanderings – and certain destitution. Should anyone happen to take the trouble to read this diary one day, it would also be a faithful mirror of the ever faster pace of my development which, for all I know, may already be in its final stage.

Saturday, 30 June 1900
After two days of dreadful boredom and physical pain, I am trying to go back to work.

I feel more and more disgusted with my second self, a no-good who rears her head from time to time. Usually, if not always, under the influence of certain purely physical factors. Better health, in other words, would clearly result in an improvement in the intellectual and spiritual side of my life.

The night before last I had a long discussion with Archivir about that perennial subject of ours, namely pleasure. I still hold on to my theory, which says that one should limit one's needs as much as one can to avoid disillusionment, as well as to avoid any dulling of the senses due to unpleasant sensations.

Archivir, on the other hand, maintains that needs must be developed, and that one must use one's last ounce of energy to satisfy them.

It occurs to me this instant to write a dissertation on the subject, to be published perhaps in *L'Athénée*. Once again I feel that I am going through a period of intellectual incubation which I think will be the most fertile of my whole life so far. Reading the *Journal des Goncourts* does me a great deal of good. I shall have to use my stay in Marseilles to read the other volumes and make notes.

I have so far opted for reading matter which focuses on feelings and the imagination. As a result, my sense of poetry has been overdeveloped at the expense of pure thought. The *Journal des Goncourts* is a work that forces one to think, and *deeply* so. I must look for other, similar books and use them for discussion and debate, while I am still surrounded by people.

I am clearly aware that certain things I do are absolutely *futile*, *stupid* and *actually bad* for my future; is my will not strong enough to stand up to my ego and prevent these things? A matter to be studied, so that I can find out how to do better.

'We now have only one main interest in life: the gratification that comes from observing reality.' (*Journal des Goncourts, vol. II*, Pierre Loti) Without that, life is boring and empty.

The Nomad

Written 30 June, 8 o'clock in the evening
The more I write and develop my story, the more I feel curiously *bored* with it, hence those nagging doubts about what possible interest it may have for the reader.

It is therefore no exaggeration to say that I can no longer make up my mind whether *Rakhil* is or is not a sickening pile of badly-edited police reports.

That is why I need to read it out loud to someone and *objectify*. Needless to say, if the book has the same effect on readers as it does on me at the moment, no one will read beyond the second page.

Everything seems so tranquil this evening, despite the mindless noise coming from the boulevards teeming with people. The sky is a pale blue with scarcely any azure in it, iridescent with light tufts of cloud . . . a grey cast over the Champel trees . . . a grey cast in the sky and a grey cast over the Salève . . . Everything is in a soft grey fog, just like my mood: I am not feeling overly emotional, but feel no enthusiasm either. All I want to do is to work in peace and develop what intelligence I have.

Such apparent egocentricity to be found on every page of this diary should not be taken for megalomania . . . Oh no . . . To begin with, loners are given to constant introspection; and I do need to compile a record that can later on give me a true image of my soul as it is today. That is the only way I shall be able to judge my present life and to see whether my character has progressed or not.

Written at Geneva, 3 July 1900, 11.30 at night
I am thinking of writing a short story, to go with *La Voie*,[14] but with very different characters: Semenov, Andreyev, Sacha in Paris.

The same night at 2 in the morning
I am not asleep. I don't feel in the least like sleeping. Downstairs I can hear the piercing screams of a Russian woman in labour. What an ominous way of making one's entrance into the world, on such a rainy night, to the sound of the mother's lugubrious wails . . . ominous and, who knows? Perhaps symbolic as well.

The first thing we do in life is weep – and how much our entrance resembles our exit, except that our exiting the world is a lot less sad than our entering it, with all the suffering and sorrow it entails!

Weep ye not for the dead, neither bemoan him: but weep sore for him that goeth away: for he shall return no more, nor see his native country.
Jeremiah 22:10

11 July, 9 o'clock in the evening
I write this after a number of awful days full of problems, arguments, painful confrontations, upsets and disillusions. I am writing positioned on top of my bunk in front of the open window, on an evening whose iridescence is an exquisite reminder of those past African nights . . . Oh, the unforgettable magic of summer sunsets over Africa's white cities and dead stretches of desert!

The Nomad

Isabelle leaves Geneva for Marseilles, where her brother Augustin and his wife, Hélène, are living in meagre accommodation.

Departure from Geneva, 14 July 1900, 7.30 p.m.
The weather is grey and stormy and dark. Where am I going? . . . ∪ *Where destiny is taking me!*

15 July, 5 o'clock in the morning
Arrival in Marseilles. Fatigue. Superb sunrise over the Crau.

A sense of Africa. My arrival has gone well.

Marseilles, 9.30 in the evening
An idea occurs to me as I come upon the following phrase in the *Journal des Goncourts*: 'finished *Manette Salomon* today.' No work of literature is ever finished in the sense that it cannot either go on or, as is more often the case, bear improvement. To finish something is to feel satisfied with it.

Despite all the chaos and my disgust those last few days in Geneva, that month of living the Russian way – for the last time in my life no doubt – will always be one of my most cherished memories.

My brief romance with Archivir also had its considerable charm, yet I have said goodbye to him forever, without hard feelings of any sort.

+ *There was nothing vulgar about these people.* That is what makes it all so painful.

'The phenomenon of malice in the domain of love, whether such malice is physical or mental, is a sure sign that civilisation is on the wane.'
Journal des Goncourts, vol. III, Pierre Loti

Marseilles, 16 July 1900
Archivir leaves me with very gentle memories that are somewhat mysterious, just like his strange personality and our strange romance.

Archivir has the Armenian's dreamy moodiness, and violent but poetic make-up. He has also acquired the Russian student's indefinable cachet I love so much, one with which I *identify*.

I do not remember ever having worked for any reason other than a sense of duty or, more importantly, inspiration. I never work to fight boredom, because the results are no good in that case. I read a lot, which usually takes care of boredom, as it does of the terrors of a sleepless night.

My present objective is the same it has always been: my intellectual and spiritual progress. As far as work in the intellectual domain goes, it may be less advanced but is much easier.

It is about time I understood that *there can be no prolonging what has come to an end, nor any resuscitating what is over and done with. Nothing can ever happen twice.* I went back to Geneva to try to live there the way I once did. Did I succeed? Quite on the contrary! I have buried it. So no doubt I am off for Ouargla. The only thing I am beginning to fear is that the sweltering heat may interfere with my work. I gather, though, that the temperature is about 40°C here today, and I do not feel any worse than I usually do. I will need to fight the certain indolence that comes with the Sahara climate in summer, not only because I will have work to do, but also for reasons of hygiene.

Yes, I do begin to see the outline of my life, even should the event of my literary efforts be crowned with success one day: it will be a sombre succession of enchanted tableaux and décors that will change at a fabulous pace . . .

I would still like to make a stab at happiness, in the form of a solitary owl's nest for myself, in some far-off place where I can be completely independent, a place to go back to and bury what loss and misfortune is still in store for me. That is what I shall try to build for myself in the middle of the desert, far away from people. I want to isolate *my soul* for months and months, without any human contact whatsoever. Above all I must avoid sharing anyone's lot from now on, whether in the form of embarrassing love affairs or friendships, merely lumping together my own concerns and interests with those of others, as they are bound to run counter to each other.[15] That will at least spare me a good deal of suffering.

I must force myself to create an inner world of thoughts and feelings which will console me in my solitude and poverty, and in the absence of aesthetic pleasures, which are too much of a luxury in my present situation.[16] I must, at all costs, put into practise my theory of diminishing my needs as much as possible. If I am reasonably settled and observe the rules of hygiene, my health should hold out.

As for my state of mind, it is now more than urgent that I get down to work. This is my only chance of earning a living now that my feeble means have been wiped out, and is also a safeguard against despondency.

I must also learn to live in the *present moment* and not, as I have so far done, only in the future, which is a natural source of pain. To live in the past and think of what was good and beautiful about it amounts to a sort of *seasoning* of the present, while the perennial wait for later, for tomorrow, is bound to result in chronic discontent that is sheer poison for one's mental outlook.

I must learn to feel *more deeply*, to see *better*, and above all, to *think*.

With the definite prospect of leaving for Africa, Isabelle is in good spirits, and lists her plans and good intentions.

18 July, 9 o'clock at night
It does look as though things have been decided at last, as though I am actually off to Africa on Saturday, after an absence of nine months. My God, if only upon reaching Ouargla I could muster the courage to set up the nest I need so much, a solitary owl's nest, and stay there for at least six months and above all, do some work there.

Tonight I will reread the whole of my novel *Rakhil*. In order to discover what I think of it, I need the one thing I have not had – an overall view. All it now needs to stand as a story is the scene with the Jewish women going for a stroll, which would amount to a half-hour's work. Before I do anything else, however, I must finish reading and annotating the *Journal des Goncourts* while I am still here.

Next, I must take note of the odd striking passage from other writers: Baudelaire, Zola.

While travelling, I must carefully write down not only *factual information*, but also my *impressions*. I must come up with an interesting and picturesque description of my crossing of the Mediterranean and journey through the ancient sites of Algeria and the Oued Rir. That will be the first thing to put on paper there.

I must also write down everything I see in the oasis; a detailed summary with as much information as possible. After that, I must start a *literary diary* about my life out there. Meanwhile, I must turn my book *Rakhil* into what it has got to be, above all else: a true work of art.

I must also, for publication in Russian, write the description of my journey through the Sahel last autumn, plus a few + *short stories*.

A gruelling workload, but that is my only road to salvation. Then, once I have *La Villa Neuve* out of the way, I shall go to Paris, if I can afford it, to lead an altogether different life there than I did before, and do everything within my power to make a success of the material I bring along.[17]

That is the only sensible plan I can make for the moment.

If, by autumn, there is a move towards Morocco, I will of course go along and take detailed notes at all times.

Yesterday, at four in the afternoon, I took the omnibus down the Cours Devilliers to the Quai de la Fraternité. I thought Marseilles looked very colourful, true to form.

I went for a long walk with Augustin, and we first stopped at the Fort Saint-Nicholas Bridge. We watched the physical exertion necessary to turn the bridge around and let through a Greek sailboat named *Eleni*. At the bow stood a man with a coarse face, in shirtsleeves and a felt hat, who kept shouting: *'Vira, vira, vira!'* to the crew heaving sternside at the capstan to try and steer the vessel.

Silhouettes of young bathers in their bathing trunks, who looked happy to be wet and naked in the sun and kept striking poses.

We crossed the old harbour by ferry below Fort Saint-Jean and paid a visit to the Quai de la Joliette, across from the Africa-bound ships.

Huge black heaps, black dust and black-looking men in rags and covered with soot; the whites of their eyes looked dirty, their mouths looked like wounds and any patch of real skin that showed through might as well have been the hideous mark of leprosy. An equally black tavern, where a sunburnt man with the face of a crook was arguing with a visibly frightened coal-docker. Back to the jetty. The horizon looked a greenish aquamarine and the sea was slightly choppy. Watched a net being pulled in between two heaving boats.

Quai du Lazaret. Back in the coal tavern, a man had asked me for a light and, already very drunk, kept singing and making a lot of noise. We saw him again on the quay, sitting on top of his cart, waving, holding forth and laughing in the midst of a crowd, under the gaze and indulgent smiles of the police who were probably biding their time to arrest him . . . something about the drunkard having crushed a soldier's leg.

We came home at eight o'clock.

Fatigue, intense headache and nausea.

Friday 20 July, 10 o'clock at night in Marseilles
Everything is finished, packed and closed . . . The only thing left here is my camp bed, which must wait till morning.

At one o'clock in the afternoon tomorrow I leave for Algiers.

The fact is, I have not really quite believed I would actually be leaving for Ouargla. So many things had stood in the way of my carrying out the daring of my plan.

My chances of success are good, for I leave well equipped. As for my mood, I feel great sadness, as I now do every time I leave this house, even though I am no more than a passing stranger in it.

Yet I also feel a glimmer of hope. I know my present mood will pass as soon as I am with my friend Eugène[18] in Algiers, when there will be new impressions for me to take in.

In any event I must work, and write, over there . . . My God, if I could only muster the energy to knuckle down and finish part at least of all I have got to do!

Would it not be a better idea to start my description of my trip through Algeria with Bône rather than Algiers? That trip will give me the material for a book, a good one I can write quickly and that can perhaps be published before *Rakhil*.

I sometimes feel so pessimistic that I look ahead with a feeling of irrational terror, as if the future can be only bad and terrifying, even though many of those dark clouds have in fact gone from my horizon.

Isabelle leaves Marseilles for North Africa on 21 July on board the *SS Eugène Pereire*, and docks at Algiers at 3 p.m. the next day. Her arrival feels like a homecoming.

Algiers, 22 July 1900, 11 o'clock at night
It was hot yesterday afternoon when I boarded the same ship I took last September. I kept staring at Augustin's outline until, when the ship tacked, it disappeared from view. I then studied the horizon. The harbour was full of the powerful red and black shapes of transatlantic steamers . . . then came the city. To begin with, when the ship was in the middle of the harbour, Marseilles looked like a delicate palette of grisailles: the grey of the smoky sky, the blue-grey tones of the mountains, the pinkish-grey ones of the rooftops, the yellowish ones of the Colline de Notre Dame . . . the silvery, lilac hues of the sea . . . while among all those shades of grey the hardy vegetation growing among the rocks provided so many dots of greenish-brown . . . The green foliage of the plane trees, the cathedral's gilded cupolas and statue of the Virgin Mary were the only things to stand out in sharp and lively contrast. Yet, once the ship was at some distance, everything looked quite different: it was all a monochrome gold, so intense one could hardly believe one's eyes.

Watched the sun go down while the sea turned stern and sombre.

Spent a peaceful night on a sternside bench. Felt truly well; woke up by about 2.45 a.m.

Saw the sun come up while sailors were putting up the canvas. First there was rosy dawn, the colour of lavender. Then a crimson disc appeared, clear-cut in outline. Slightly above it were the lacy shapes of pink clouds outlined in gold.

All night long I had the feeling of mysterious well-being I always get when peacefully asleep with the ship's lights shining over my head.

I will continue this report tomorrow.

Algiers, 23 July

Oh, the sense of bliss I had this evening of knowing that I am *back*, once I was inside those solemn mosques and in the ancient hustle and bustle of the Arab *tabadji* in the rue Jénina!

Oh, that extraordinary feeling of intoxication I had tonight, in the peaceful shadows of the great al-Jadid Mosque during the *icha* prayer!

I feel I am coming back to life again . . . ∪ *Lead us along the straight path, the one taken by those to whom you have been generous!*

10.30 p.m.

For a long, long time all you could see of the Algerian coast was Matifou, steeped in a world of grey vapours. Next, one could see the Algiers triangle, with the old part of town looking like an avalanche of snow. This was followed by a splendid view of the entire panorama in full daylight.

After a very brief moment spent in my room with Eugène, he left and I went exploring by myself. My hat bothered me though, for it cut me off from Muslim life. I went back to don my fez, and went out again with Ahmed, the manservant, to go to the al-Kabir Mosque first. It was so cool and peaceful there underneath those white, serrated arcades. Went to greet the mosque's *wakil*, a venerable old man who sat in a side niche writing on his knee. Nothing surprises him any longer. He has no misplaced or indiscreet curiosity.

I then went to that charming blue-tinted *zawyia* of Sidi el Rahman and stood for a while in the cool shade facing the *mihrab* upon the thick rugs. Drank some jasmine-scented water from the earthenware pitcher on the windowsill.

The *zawyia* is a veritable jewel of great beauty, and I will go back there before I leave Algiers.

Dashes of an unvarnished bluish-white among the greenery in the Jardin Marengo. Smelt a sweet and heady fragrance I could not place as I walked through it, of flowers I could not identify.

Had supper at Al-Haj-Muhammad's, on the corner of the rue Jénina. I felt *intensely* the joy of returning, of being back once again in this African land to which I feel tied not only by the best memories of my life, but also by that strange attraction I have always felt for it, even before I had seen it, years ago in the monotonous Villa.

I felt so happy sitting at a table in an old dive; a feeling impossible to describe, one I have never felt anywhere but in Africa.

How much Arabs resemble each other! At Haj-Muhammad's yesterday I saw men come in whom I thought I had known in earlier days, in Bône, Batna, or in the South . . . but not in Tunisia, where they look very different. Why is that so? Because Islam leaves no room for individual development, or because it has a levelling influence? Both no doubt.

After dinner this evening, I went to say the *icha* prayer in the al-Jadif Mosque, which is less beautiful than the two others, but the soaring sense of Islam was superb.

The place was cool and dark as I went in, and a handful of oil-lamps were the only source of light.

A feeling of ancient Islam, tranquil and mysterious.

Stood for a long time near the *mihrab*. Somewhere far behind us, a clear, fresh, high voice went up, a dreamlike voice that took turns with that of the elderly *imam* standing in the *mihrab* where he recited the *fatiha* with his quavering voice.

Standing next to each other, we all prayed as we listened to the exhilarating yet solemn exchange between those two voices. The one in front of us sounded old and hoarse, but gradually grew louder till it was strong and powerful, while the other one seemed to come from somewhere high up in the mosque's dark reaches as it sang triumphantly in regular intervals of its unshakeable, radiant faith in Allah and his Prophet . . . I felt almost in ecstasy, my chest tightening and my heart soaring up towards the heavenly regions that the second voice seemed to be coming from in a tone of melancholy joy, utterly convinced and at peace.

Oh, to lie upon the rugs of some silent mosque, far from the mindless noise of city life, and, eyes closed, the soul's gaze turned heavenwards, listen to Islam's song forever!

I remember the time I wandered around till daybreak one night last year, looking for Ali and the poet. I ended up by the Morkad ruins at the foot of the minaret, where the windows were all lit up. In the dead silence of the Tunis night I heard the muezzin's voice. It sounded infinitely mysterious as it placidly sang, ∪ *Prayer is better than sleep*, and those rhythmical notes still echo in my ears.

After the *icha* prayer, which is a lovely moment of the day, I went out for an aimless stroll. Upon my return around ten o'clock, I spent some time in front of a small shop in a narrow street. The place was lit by an oil lamp. A guitar, pipestems and decoration in the form of paper cut-outs.

The shopkeeper was stretched out on an oval mat in front, a dark, rather handsome, indifferent-looking man whose gestures were infinitely slow, as though his mind were elsewhere. Might that have been due to *kef*?[19]

Bought a small pipe and some *kef*.

That more or less sums up what I did yesterday.

The day of my arrival has turned out to be an incomparable one.

Isabelle sets off on 27 July for the Souf region of the South, travelling in the notoriously rough third-class train carriages from Constantine to Touggourt, and from there as a nomad, sleeping on the sand beneath the stars at night, accompanied by a guide, Habib. She decides to make her base in El Oued, an oasis town that she visited the year before.

The Nomad

El Merayer, 30 July 1900
Left Algiers on 27 July, eight o'clock in the morning.

Frame of mind fairly good, but spoiled by the presence of Lieutenant Lagrange's mistress, a horrible, revolting creature.

At Sidi Amram, I lay down near some burning dried *djerid*, next to a French soldier who had turned up out of nowhere; drank some coffee, felt weak, slightly feverish. The fire's flames cast a strange red light upon the mud walls, underneath a roof of stars.

Touggourt, 31 July 1900, Tuesday noon
I am sitting in the near total obscurity of the dining room, to get away from the innumerable flies in my own room.

If the Arab Bureau[20] has no objection, I shall be off for El Oued this evening and try to settle down there. All things considered, my health will run much less of a risk over there than at Ouargla.

I am pleased to find the desert's torrid heat does not bother me too much, even though I am not feeling altogether normal because I am worn out by my journey and recent late nights. I can now work and think, however. In fact, it is only today that I am beginning to recover. I will not really feel well, though, until the day I settle in El Oued and all is quiet around me.

I am also beginning to realise the thrift and the strength of will it takes to avoid squandering the little money I have left. I must remember that I have come to the desert, not to indulge in last year's *dolce far niente*, but to work, and that this journey of mine could turn either into a ghastly shipwreck of my future, utter failure, or prove a prelude towards my salvation, both materially and for my soul, depending on whether I can manage everything properly or not.

I have an altogether charming memory of Algiers, from the first night to the last in particular. The last evening I went with Mokhtar and Abdel Kaim Oulid Issa to a tobacconist's on the Plateau Saulières. We had a rather lively conversation, and then went for a melancholy stroll along the quays. Ben Elimaur, Mokhtar and Zarrouk, the medical student, softly sang wistful Algerian cantilenas. I had many moments of intense life, of fully Oriental life, at Algiers. The long journey I made in third class, almost alone with someone as juvenile and young as Mokhtar, also had its charm.

I have said farewell to the big blue sea, perhaps for a long time to come. I travelled through wild Kabyle territory and a landscape of jagged rocks. Then, after the grey hills of the Portes de Fer, came the desolate high argillaceous plateaux looking vaguely gilded by fields cultivated way up there by Arabs – long, tawny-silver dots upon the landscape's oranges and ochres. The plains at Borj-bou-Arérij offer a more desperately sad and dreary spectacle than I have ever come across.

Saint Arnaud looks like Batna. It is a large village lost among the high plateaux of Cheonïya country. Yet Saint Arnaud, *Elelma* in Arabic, is a verdant spot. Its gardens are like those of the Randon column at Bône.

The Cadi is a noble and serene old man, who belongs to another age. Alas! In ten, twenty years' time, will today's young Algerians resemble their fathers and be as steeped as they are in the solemn serenity of their

Islamic faith? The Cadi's son, Si Ali, seems at first sight to be sleepy and heavy. Yet he is an intelligent man who cares about the public interest. Si Ihsan, who is of Turkish origin, is a man whose charm lies in his candour.

Had a pleasantly intense sense of old Africa and Bedouin country the first night at Elelma: there was the distant sound of dogs barking all night long, and the crowing of the rooster. Serenity, sweet melancholia and carefree living.

Felt seduced all over again by the heady sight of a desert sunrise as I travelled from Biskra to Touggourt. . . and also at Bir Sthil yesterday, when the old caretaker gave us coffee, and then at El Moggar this morning when I sat by the fire.

Crossed the lugubrious Ourlana oasis around two in the morning last night: vast gardens enclosed by clay walls, *segniyas* reeking of saltpetre, humidity and fever. The mud houses all seemed to be in a curious state of slumber.

At Sidi Amram I stretched out on the ground by a fire that was burning dried *djerids*. The sand felt warm and the sky was ablaze with countless stars.

Oh Sahara, menacing Sahara, hiding your dark and beautiful soul in bleak, desolate emptiness! Oh yes, I love this country of sand and stone, this country of camels and primitive men and vast, treacherous salt-flats.

Between Mraïer and El Berd last night I saw bizarre and fetishistic, vaguely human forms garbed in red and white rags, at the exact spot where a Muslim was assassinated a few years ago. It is a forlorn monument of sorts put up in memory of the death of that man, who lies buried at Touggourt.

Borj Terdjen, 1 August, 7 a.m.
Set off from Taïbet at 4.45 yesterday afternoon on N'Tardjallah's mule with Al-Haj-Muhammad. Reached Mguetla by nine o'clock.

As the sun was setting, I saw the tawny dunes transform into an incomparably brilliant shade of gold, while behind me was an infinite stretch of white, translucent, almost blue in the light of the waxing moon. An unbelievably delicate purity of colours.

In spite of slight fatigue, I had an excellent impression of the first encampment.

An almost cold wind blew during the night, and in the dunes a murmur like that of the sea. A feeling of desolation, infinitely sad, for no reason at all.

Magnificent sunrise. Arose at 4 a.m. A pristine sky, cool and rather strong north-easterly wind.

Set off at five o'clock. Struck camp and made coffee in the dunes. The mail coach caught up with us. Rode a camel till Terdjen. Arrived at eight.

Excellent frame of mind. State of health, ditto.

How glad I am I left Europe and decided – yesterday – to choose El Oued for my base. Provided my health holds up, I must stay at El Oued as long as is possible. Above all, I pray this time will not be wasted, from all points of view, but especially vis-à-vis my intellectual and spiritual development and literary endeavours.

El Oued, 4 August 1900, 7 a.m.
As I finished writing in my diary at Terjen, I sat down on my bed, facing the door.

I had a sense of well-being and profound bliss in being there, that was almost beyond explanations.

Siesta interrupted by children and goats.

Left with the mail coach around 2.30 p.m. Intense heat. Did not feel well. Mounted the camel once more. Reached Mouïet-el-Caïd by *maghreb* (6 p.m.).

A sleepless night. By about 2 a.m. a dull, flat, red light rose up over the dune. In the dawn's uncertain glimmer, a fiery Lucifer then began his triumphant ascent. As the Arabs put it, ∪ *he went up to the borj.*

Woke up Habib. Lit a fire and made coffee. By 4 a.m. off to Ourmes, where we arrived by half-past seven. Crossed the biggest dune and came upon several dead camels, one of which was a recent casualty.

Ourmes. Siesta in the park. An enchanted sight.

Did not sleep well because of inevitable flies and hot *burnous*. Set off again by 4.30 p.m. Was at El Oued around *maghreb*.

Dismounted in front of Habib's house, in the middle of the street.

Went to see a house that belongs to a *caïd*, on the town square opposite the *borj*. Rented it. Have started moving in.

The evening of my arrival, a beautiful ride on mules. A night that looked transparent on the white sand. A deep garden, fast asleep in darkness. Nothing but things cool and mellow all around.

Here I am, finally arrived at the goal which, as a plan, seemed a little fanciful. Now it is done, and I must muster all the energy I can and set to work on the story of my travels, with Marseilles as the first chapter.

I am far away from all people, far from civilisation and its hypocritical shams. I am alone, on the soil of Islam, out in the desert, free and in excellent condition. Apart from my health, the results of my undertaking now depend only on me . . .

3.30 in the afternoon
I am beginning to feel inert, for my luggage has not turned up and I cannot get on with my house and life . . .

Habib's house. A square building of unbleached mud, in one of the winding streets paved with fine sand, not far from the dune.

Off in a corner is a small, dark goat with an amulet around its neck. Habib's many brothers come and go. The old man's wife, tall and slim, is dressed in long white veils, a veritable mountain on top of her head: braids of black hair, braids and tassels made of red wool, and in her ears heavy iron rings held up by cords tied to the hair. To go out, she throws a blue veil over it all. A strange, lean and ageless figure with a sunburnt skin and doleful black eyes.

An old *kef*-smoking fellow who is off in a sweet dream of his own.

Temperatures will soon start going down. There is already a little gust of wind from time to time.

To sum things up, I have not yet embarked upon my new way of life. Too much of it is still unsettled.

Isabelle has met Slimène Ehnni, an Arab soldier of the Spahi regiment taken over by the French Army. They

begin a relationship and are forced, owing to the delicately balanced relations between the European and Arab communities and the recent rebel uprisings, to conduct their meetings in secret, at night. Their love is fulfilling both sexually and intellectually for Isabelle.

El Oued, Thursday 9 August 7.30 p.m.
For the time being there is nothing durable about this Arab lifestyle of mine, which is indolent, but in no dangerous way, for I know it will not last. My little dwelling is beginning to look like a household. I am still short of money, though.

I must avoid borrowing any from the *bach-adel*, for he is clearly no altruist.

A few days from now I expect to change my lifestyle altogether.

Every evening, Slimène and I go to Bir R'Arby. We cross the snow-white sands that seem almost translucent in the moonlight. We pass the gloomy silhouettes of the Christian cemetery: high grey walls with a black cross on top . . . the impression is a lugubrious one. From there we go up a low hill, and in a deep and narrow valley we see the garden, which is no different from any other Souafa garden: its shape is that of a funnel which opens up on one side to the paths leading into it and to the wells. At the bottom stand the highest palm trees, the smaller ones grow near the wells.

In the bluish-green light of the moon they look diaphanous, like delicate, feathery plumes. Between their handsome, chiselled trunks lies the odd verdant stretch of melons, watermelons and fragrant basil.

The water is clear and cool. The well's primitive iron frame makes a squeaking noise that already sounds familiar; the goatskin *oumara* fell in and briefly made lapping noises in the well's dark interior before surfacing again, dripping wet. I threw my *chechiya* down on the pristine sand, soaked my head in the *oumara* and took a few greedy gulps of water. It was refreshing and cool, with that feeling of almost agonised sensuality which cold water gives here. After that we stretched out on the sand.

All is silent in the blue night; the palm trees' stiff foliage rustles mysteriously in the perennial wind of the Souf, which vaguely sounds like a wind at sea.

Slowly and laboriously, we head back to the sleeping town and that white house that is now my home, God knows for how long . . .

Isabelle comments upon the difficulties, 'the truly terrible possibilities', that face herself and Slimène at this time: the social and political ramifications that would confront them should they be betrayed by the few that they have chosen to trust with the secret of their affair. She refers to the Arab anti-colonial rebellions: the 'local indiscretions'.

The other night I spent in a large garden that belongs to the Hacheich Caïdat, west of El Oued, together with Slimène.[21] It is a very deep, funnel-shaped oblong, set between towering walls of white sand on whose ridges stand low hedges made of dried *djerid* to keep the sand at bay. Not a soul was breathing in the palm trees' warm shadows.

We sat down near a well where I had unsuccessfully tried to draw water with a torn *oumara*. We both felt deeply saddened, and in my case the thought of trouble due to local indiscretions loomed large in my mind.

My sadness is an inscrutable well of melancholy, unanalysable, without any known cause and which is the very essence of my soul. My soul has aged, alas. It has ceased to delude itself and I can only smile at Slimène's dreams. His soul is still young, he thinks that earthly love is eternal. He also talks of what will happen in a year's, in *seven years*' time. Yet what would be the use of telling him, of making him feel sad and hurting him? That will all happen by itself the day we go our inevitable separate ways.

It is a fact, though, that for some time now I have known about life. As for love, on that score there is not only no illusion left in me, but also no *desire* for illusions, no urge to try to make these things last which are only sweet and good because they are ephemeral . . . But then, this kind of thing is so personal, so much *my problem*, that it is impossible to explain it clearly, let alone to make anyone else understand me. The price of experience is life's great sorrows, but it cannot be *shared*.

After an hour spent talking, with tears in our eyes, about the truly terrible possibilities that might occur, we went to sleep under the palm trees on top of our *burnous*, using a thickness of sand for a pillow.

Slept till about 2.30 a.m. In the rising pre-dawn chill, we laboriously retraced our steps up the path through the dunes, and went back to the Hacheich Caidat. A maze of tiny alleyways reeking heavily of saltpetre, rather like the Oued Rir oases. We crossed the marketplace, which was deserted except for a few camels and their drivers, asleep by the great well's iron frame.

Isabelle grows frustrated with the amount that she is sleeping in the day, catching up on that she misses in the nights spent with Slimène.

Rode the bad white horse last night, taking the road to Kouïnine through El Oued's tiny suburbs, where black and white goats graze on top of the roofs of *zéribas* made of *djerid*.

The dune had that pale look but was turning more and more golden, the fiery, metallic sheen it gets just before the *maghreb*. The shadows lengthened out of all proportion. Everything then turned a violent red, with the dunetops contrasting a bluish or a greenish violet, in an incredible variety of shades. To the west, in the direction of Kouïnine and Touggourt, the sun was a veritable ball of blood sinking in a blaze of gold and crimson. The slopes of the dunes seemed to be on fire below the ridges, in colours that deepened from one moment to the next. Once the sun's disc had vanished in the distance, everything first went through a palette of shades of purple before turning white again, the Souf's dull white that is so blinding at noon.

This morning the sky looked dark and cloudy, a most unexpected sight in this land of implacably blue skies and tyrannical sunshine.

The fact is that for the time being my time is not being put to good use. The siesta hour has a lot to do with that. It is the same inertia that overcomes me every time I settle in a new place, especially when I am meant to stay for a certain length of time. That is bound to pass, though.

A fairly strong sirocco since this morning. The sand is flying and the air feels heavy. They say there will only be about twenty more days of great heat.

For the moment I feel in top form, and except for the occasional bout of lassitude, have never felt so well.

I would like to start working. That would mean getting up for reveille, though, at the very least, and not going back to bed after Slimène has left. The reason I do, alas, is from sheer boredom and the fact that I have nothing to do. I must go out right after reveille, visit the gardens and go for the occasional morning ride, on whatever horse happens to be available.

Spent a quarter of an hour taking administrative measures against the swarms of flies in my two rooms. The day will come when I will cherish the memory of such small chores in this simple lifestyle. To progress, though, I must make sure I am not living *elsewhere* in my mind, in a perpetual state of *expectation*. Yes, I must accept the present as it is and heed Eugène's advice, that is to say, try to see the inevitable good side of things.

Oh, if my present way of life could last, if Slimène could continue to be the good friend and brother he is right now. And if he could share more in the local side of life and get to work as soon as the weather starts to cool!

When a girl gets married over here she is taken to her husband on a man's back. To see his wife, the husband must hide for seven nights, come after the *maghreb* and leave before the morning.

Obviously a vestige of the abductions of earlier days.

18 August 1900, 3.30 p.m.
Went riding by myself last night, through the little townships all along the road to Touggourt.

Went through Teksebet. A melancholy, derelict-looking place, virtually deserted, where ruins crumble with every step.

Headed back for El Oued by sundown. Watched the sand pour down the dunes in a constant stream, like a silent ocean's pure white waves. Out west, the top of a large, pointed dune seemed to be smoking, like a volcano. The sun, which first looked yellow in the midst of sulphurous vapours, then slowly took on the usual lavish colours of its nightly apotheosis.

Getting in the saddle yesterday I heard nearby wails, of the kind that is the Arab way of broadcasting someone's death. The daughter of Salah the Spahi, young Abdel Kader's sister, had died. Today, I saw Salah smile as he played with his little boy in a shop in the marketplace.

The little girl was buried in the hot sand yesterday at *maghreb*. She was swallowed up by the eternal night, like one of those meteors seen flashing through this land's infinite sky.

'I do not believe in it [death]; *it is a sombre passage we all encounter at some time in our lives. It frightens many people who have a childish fear of the dark.*

As for myself, on the three or four occasions that I have come close to it, I saw a tiny light on the other side of that Eternal Chasm.'

Une Année dans le Sahel, Eugène Fromentin

The Nomad

Written at El Oued, 17 September 1900, noon
 Yes, there is indeed a tiny light on the other side of that Eternal Chasm.

Isabelle uses the small amount of money sent to her by Augustin to buy a horse and names him Souf, after the region. She derives great pleasure and solace in her lone rides across the sands, but financial difficulties owing to complications in her legal claim to her mother's and Trophimowsky's estates are beginning to take their toll.

Monday, 9 October 1900, 9 o'clock in the morning
Shortly after the *maghreb* last night, rode Souf by the back of the café through the white, sandy streets beside houses that are half in ruin.

 The bright red sun had just set behind the dunes along the road to Touggourt. A few moments earlier, just as the sun had been about to disappear, I had spotted the silhouettes of two Arabs clothed in white standing on top of the little dune where the lime kiln is; they looked as if set against a heavenly light. The impression was a biblical one, and I suddenly felt as if transported back to the ancient days of primitive humanity, when the great light-giving bodies in the sky had been the object of veneration . . .

 At that frontier between town and desert, I was reminded of those autumn and winter sunsets in the land of exile, when the great snow-capped Jura mountains seemed to come closer and turn into an expanse of pale blonde and bluish hues.

 It is chilly in the morning now. The light has changed colour. We no longer have the flat glare of stifling summer days. The sky is now a violent shade of blue, pure and invigorating.

Everything has come to life again, and so has my soul. Yet, as always, I also feel a boundless sadness, an inarticulate longing for something I cannot describe, a nostalgia for *some other place* for which I have no name.

For several days now, intellectual endeavour has seemed less repellent to me than it did this summer, and I think I shall go on writing. The wellspring does not seem to have run dry.

I have gone through a period of financial difficulties and problems that have not yet run their course. The immediate future certainly looks drab, and I cannot tell how long my stay here in the desert will last. For the moment I do not feel up to taking off and parting from Slimène forever, even if I could afford to do so. And why should I?

I feel a tranquil heart is mine at last; the same cannot be said for any peace of mind, alas!

How amazing are my changes in mood! A moment ago, as I was about to start jotting down these notes, I was in one of those moods of melancholy lucidity that take hold of me on certain bright and luminous mornings as I gallop along the road to Amiche through the *land of the graves*. As I am finishing them just now, I have that familiar feeling of unreasonable crankiness that makes me snap so rudely at anyone who speaks to me.

Changed lodgings the evening of 14 October.

Isabelle moves to a house in the old Jewish quarter of El Oued. Her new set-up is fairly domestic, with a servant, Khalifa, an orderly, Biskri, a goat and her horse, Souf. Slimène joins her whenever he can. The apparent tranquillity of this period is interrupted by lapses of the household – servants included – into frequent, collective drunkenness, culminating after one binge in Isabelle's smashing down her front door. Thereafter, Isabelle vows to try to lead a more sober life.

El Oued, 27 October 1900, 9 p.m.
Went to Amiche on the 17th, to look for Sidi El Hussein.

It was chilly when we left at around six that morning. Arrived in no time at all at Sheikh Blanc's great *zawyia*, which seemed quite empty and deserted, near those vast and gloomy cemeteries. Set off again with two manservants, and passed long strings of houses and gardens, whose helter-skelter patterns looked quite picturesque.

The *zawyia* of Sidi el Imann, a lonely and derelict building, stands on a ridge in the dunes where it is surrounded by ruins and a beautiful, lush garden. I turned left there and crossed the Chaambas' colony. Ran into Gosenelle and the doctor, and then into two Chaambas carrying one of their brethren to his final resting place upon a stretcher.

Isabelle visits Sidi El Hussein ben Brahim, sheikh of the *zawyia* of Guémar and eldest son of the late Sidi Brahim, *marabout* and Grand Sheikh of the brotherhood of the Qadrya, the oldest mystical Sufi order within Islam. El Hussein initiates Isabelle into the order, an unprecedented acceptance for a European.

Found Sidi El Hussein[22] at long last at the far end of Ras-el-Amiche, facing the infinite stretches of sand that lead to the distant Sudan.

Spent the siesta hour with the sheikh in a narrow and primitive room that had no windows. It was vaulted and had sand on the floor, and it constituted the whole interior of the house, which stands all by itself.[23]

A strange figure showed up, an almost black Southerner with burning eyes who suffers from a form of epilepsy that makes him strike at anyone who touches or frightens him . . . yet he is gentle and very congenial.

Left at about three o'clock with the sheikh for the Chaambas colony. Set off again by myself around 3.15. Reached the cemeteries located to the right of Amiche by sundown. At the *maghreb* hour, stopped on the dune that overlooks the Ouled-Touati.

On my left, the plains looked pink, and in the village I saw a few women in blue rags and an oddly shaped red dromedary. Utter peace and silence all around . . . Returned home around 5.15 p.m.

I have now reached a state of destitution that for quite some time has been inevitable. Yet, in bringing me to El Oued, Providence seems to have wanted to spare me worse suffering in other places. Who knows, it may be that all these strokes of bad luck will merely serve to forge my character and pull me out of the indolent *indifference* that often comes over me when the future is at stake.

May God help me succeed! So far I have always survived unscathed even the worst and most perilous of pitfalls. Fate will not quite forsake me just yet, perhaps. + *The ways of the Lord are inscrutable.*

4 November 1900

Took Souf this morning to go into the dunes and gardens that lie between the road to Touggourt and the one to Debila. Steep paths leading to the dunetops overlooking deep gardens down below.

It rained last night; the sand was wet and yellow and gave off a nice, cool, slightly salty smell.

On the monotonous hillsides grows the odd succulent, a light green and spindly sort of sedum. In the gardens, the carrots and peppers look like bright green carpets underneath palm trees that have shed all that grey dust.

Everything is coming to life again and this African autumn is quite like the summers we used to have over in the land of exile, especially at sundown.

My life remains the same, monotonous and devoid of any real changes. It has even become very sheltered, for I spend part of my time inside my house – which I consider as no more than temporary quarters as we are about to move – and part in Mansour's place. The rest of the time I go to the house of Abdel Kader, of whom I am growing truly fond. If I could come up with the odd book in his place, I would feel very gratified indeed.

As for Slimène, nothing has changed, other than the fact that I grow fonder of him by the day. He is truly becoming a member of my family, or rather *is my family*. May that last forever, even over here among these perennially grey sands!

I occasionally stand still and can only marvel at my astounding destiny . . . To be in an oasis somewhere in the desert, after all those twists of fate and grandiose dreams of mine! And how will it all end?

El Oued, early November 1900

Sin, that is to say *evil*, is man's natural condition, as it is of all living beings.

Whatever *good* we do is often no more than an illusion. Should it happen to be *real*, it is merely the result of a victory we have ever so slowly and laboriously won over our own natures which, rather than helping us do the right thing, are constantly in our way . . .

El Oued, 1 December 1900, at the house of Salah ben Taliba

The beginning of this month of December is curiously reminiscent of the same time in that deadly year of 1897.[24] Same weather, same violent wind lashing against my face. In those days, though, I had the vast, grey Mediterranean for a horizon, breaking furiously against the black rocks with a deafening, cataclysmic sound. I was still so young, and even though recently bereaved, I still had a full measure of *joie de vivre*.

Since then, however, everything has changed, everything; I have aged and matured thanks to this strange destiny of mine.

Yes, everything has changed indeed. Augustin has found his haven at long last, and it does look as if he is meant never to leave it again. After all those ups and downs and twists of fate have settled down at last, however oddly.

I could never be content with the genteel pleasures of city life in Europe. My idea of heading for the desert to satisfy my need for both adventure and peace required courage, but was inspired. I've found domestic happiness, and far from diminishing, it seems to grow stronger every day.

Only politics threatens it . . . But alas! ∪ *Allah alone knows what is hidden in the sky and the earth!* and no one can predict the future.

Barely two weeks ago I went to meet my beloved in the night, as far as the area south of Kouïnine. I rode Souf in a darkness so dense it made my head spin.

Lost my way several times. Had strange impressions down in those plains, where the horizon seems to rise in the shape of dunes, and villages look like hedges made of *djerid*.

I was thinking about the passage in *Aziyadé*[25] about Istanbul graves lit by dim and solitary lights, when I suddenly spotted the gate to the Teksebet cemetery's dome.

Every afternoon for several days in a row I have been along the road to Debila, either with Khalifa Taher or by myself. One day, as I was on a solitary outing, I had a strange feeling of *familiarity,* of a return to a past that was dead and buried. Going through the shott I stopped my horse beneath the palm trees. I closed my eyes, and listening to the sound of the wind rustling in the foliage, I was off in a dream. I felt as if I were back in the big woods along the Rhône and in the Parc Sarrazin on a mellow summer evening. The illusion was almost perfect. It was not long before a sudden movement of Souf's brought me back to reality, though. I opened my eyes . . . an endless succession of grey dunes rolled out before me, and above my head the foliage rustled on the tough *djerids*.

At the foot of the dune behind our house, next to an enclosure containing three low palm trees, stands a small

African-looking mosque built of ochre-coloured plaster that looks like mud. It only has a tiny, fortified dome, a *koubba*, ovoid in shape. Behind it stands a splendid date palm which, seen from our rooftop, seems to grow out of the *koubba* itself.

Yesterday, I went up there at *maghreb* time. In the blaze of the setting sun I could see grey silhouettes drenched in scarlet light move by the post office in the distance. While the little dome seemed to be on fire and the muezzin's slow and languorous voice recited the evening prayer in the direction of every corner in the sky, men came down the dune on my right-hand side in the splendour of that melancholy hour.

Poignant memories of the end of the + *White Spirit's* life have come to haunt me these last few days.

Isabelle is living in poverty, the weather is bad, and her house has no fireplace or glass in the windows. The Villa Neuve legacy is still unconcluded and she is rapidly running up debts.

El Oued, Friday 14 December 1900, 2 p.m.
It is getting colder all the time. There was a thick fog last night that reminded me of those misty days in the *land of exile*.

I am going to have a hard time getting through the winter without heat or money . . . yet I am not at all anxious to leave this curious place.

I sat in the courtyard of the Elakbab *Zawyia*, and marvelled at the strange scene I saw there: the unusual-looking heads of sunburnt Chaambas from Troud in the South, half-covered in grey veils, the expression on

their almost black faces was so spirited that they looked
ferocious . . . in the dilapidated courtyard of the *zawyia*
they all gravitated around that huge red-haired sheikh
with his soft, blue eyes[26] . . . His is a destiny that is
becoming stranger every day, even more so than mine!

Yet there is one thing I miss, and that is those dreams
of mine about being a writer . . . will they ever come
true, alas?

**It is Ramadan, the Muslim month of fasting, and Isabelle
attends a desert *fantasia*. She is fascinated by Si Hachemi
ben Brahim (Si Lachmi), sheikh and brother to El Hussein.**

My best memory of the South will no doubt be of that
memorable day, 3 December, when I had the good
fortune to witness a breathtaking sight, the return of
the great *marabout* Si Mahmoud Lachmi, a fascinating
figure impossible to describe, whose strange personality
had attracted me in Touggourt. Si Lachmi is meant to
have a strange hold over adventurous souls.[27] On that
pure and iridescent winter morning, it was a rare and
heady experience to be engulfed by gunpowder, wild
strains of music coming from the *nefsaoua des bendar*,
frenetic shouts from the crowd welcoming one of the
Prophet's descendants, and the frantic horses in the
midst of all that smoke and uproar . . .

24 December 1900 (Ramadan)
I have been feeling ill and weak, have had to cope with
the side effects of fasting, to say nothing of the far more
serious matter of my financial problems, yet these
Ramadan nights and mornings have quite unexpectedly

brought me moments of a quiet and pleasurable serenity that borders on joy.

I see clearly now that the only way to lead a quiet life – which is not to say a happy one, for illness, misery and death exist – is to turn one's back on mankind with the exception of a small handful of chosen ones, still making sure one does not *depend on them* in any way.

Arab society as found in the big cities, unhinged and vitiated as it is by its contact with a foreign world, does not exist down here. As for French civilisation . . . from what I have been able to glean from the Infantry Lieutenant and especially the doctor, it has certainly gone downhill down here.

On 14 January 1901, an official military decision is made to transfer Slimène to Batna. The French authorities hope that this will force Isabelle – a controversial figure in her cross-dressing, her religious affiliation and her close association with the Arab community – out of the Souf.

Isabelle and Slimène struggle to meet their debts and Isabelle writes to Augustin that she is 'so thin that it hurts to lie on my bed' and is suffering from cystitis.

28 January 1901, 8 o'clock in the morning
Once again, all has been shattered and destroyed: my indolent way of life has come to an abrupt end! No more of the blissful serenity we had both begun to take for granted.

On the evening of the 23rd we chanced to find out that Slimène was about to be relieved of his duties and sent back to Batna. It was a moment of unspeakable anguish and of near despair.

Nor was that all. To add to our sorrow at the thought of imminent departure and the hardships of life in Batna, was our distress over our financial situation and the hundred francs worth of debts, a sum we could not even begin to pay.

A gloomy, sleepless night, spent drinking and smoking *kef*.

The next morning, I made a quick and worried visit to Si Lachmi. Found him surrounded by pilgrims about to leave for the sheikh of Nefta's great *ziara*. Spent over an hour mouthing banalities at him, while my mind was elsewhere and I had a lump in my throat. In the end I took the sheikh aside and agreed to come back with Slimène after the *maghreb* hour. I felt limp with exhaustion as I went home at full trot, standing in the stirrups.

Found Slimène in a half-demented state, looking haggard and no longer aware of what he was doing.

Went out on Souf that night shortly before *maghreb*.

We later had a sinister ride by the uncertain light of a waxing moon. Very much afraid that Slimène might fall off his horse, anxious to know what the sheikh would do for us. We arrived at last, responded with impatience to the repeated greetings of Guezzoun and other servants, and found ourselves seated all alone before the sheikh in the vast room with sand on the floor and low, powerful arches. A candle lit the great red carpet we were sitting on, which left the corners of the room in blurry shadows.

There was a great and ponderous silence. I felt that my poor Rouh'[28] was unable to speak at all, and I myself felt as if someone were strangling me. Then I saw tears coming into Rouh's eyes and wanted to weep too.

Upset as I was, I tried for a long time to tell the sheikh about our predicament. He said nothing, looking overcome, as if his mind were elsewhere.

In the end the sheikh and I exchanged a glance. I tried to make mine as meaningful as possible in drawing his attention to Rouh', who was burning with fever and about to faint. The sheikh stood up and went into his house, and none too soon, for Rouh's eyes had started to glaze over with fever.

A moment later the sheikh came back and put 170 francs in front of Rouh', saying: 'God will pay the rest.'

Then, without saying anything, without even taking the notes, Rouh' looked at them and began to laugh, a crazed laugh, which terrified both the sheikh and me . . . a silent laugh, which was sadder to see than any tears. I fearfully wondered whether he wasn't going to lose his sanity completely.

I went out for some air. In the distance, the dunes along the road to Taïbet Gueblia slept in the wan light of the moon. From the rocky sand in front of me rose the eerie outlines of the little graveyard for the sheikh's children. Many an innocent creature lies asleep there; barely do these young souls come to life than they are whisked off again into the netherworld's dark, mysterious reaches. No sooner do their earthly eyes take in the sterile dunes along this vast horizon than they are dimmed at once.

I stopped among the piles of sand heaped up against the thick and heavily buttressed wall, and in that utter silence I saw a nocturnal animal I could not identify –

perhaps a little desert fox – shoot by quite close to me. I raised my eyes to heaven and, on impulse, recited the *fahita* under my breath. I also implored the Emir of Saints whose rosary I carry and was holding tightly in my hand.

I went back indoors. We left, feeling lighter of heart but wistful all the same.

We were afraid we might lose our way among those vast stretches of cemetery and wan-looking dunes. We did make our way home, though, via the village that lies to the east of the Ouled-Touati. As we came through the narrow path that overlooks the Hama Ayechi garden, the sight we saw was a curious one: the palm trees below us were all asleep in the shadows, yet there was the odd ray of silvery, occasionally vaguely pink light shining through their trunks. Very low over the western horizon, the moon's crescent was about to dip below the vast expanse of dunes overlooking the Jewish cemetery.

It was nearly ten o'clock, and there was not a sound to break the silence in all that solitude and desolation.

An atmosphere of mystery surrounded us on all sides, and we were both keenly aware of it. We did not speak, but listened to the muffled sound of our horses' hooves upon the road's well-trodden sand.

The moon was setting as we entered the Ouled-Ahmed graveyard, and for an instant the only things visible by the great dune's ridge were the crescent's two red points, a strange and disquieting sight; then they were gone and there was nothing but night and darkness.

We hardly made any headway for fear of stumbling and falling, as the road is littered with graves. When we had set off after the *maghreb* on Friday night, there were lamps burning all through the cemetery in tiny grey necropolises, wan little flames in the falling dusk. But now, everything was in shadow; the lights were out and the graves slumbered in darkness. Oh, the thought of leaving this place and perhaps never seeing it again!

These days so full of sorrow, anguish and uncertainty have made me realise just how much I love this part of the world; the loss of this land will be a bitter one – its sun, its sand, its lush gardens and the winds that have fashioned its dunes, covering them with cloud after cloud of sand for century after monotonous century.

I have studied those curious cemeteries, in particular the one south of Tarzout, its tombs like pointed bell jars, tiny *koubbas* in the shape of fortified towers, and a picturesque profusion of necropolises that surrounds the twin cities of Tarzout and Guémar.

Had no trouble finding Sidi El Hussein's dilapidated *zawyia*. Had a depressing conversation, in a shabby-looking room that leads out to a vast courtyard littered with stones in all sorts of odd shapes.

By the time I went into the outer courtyard, I spotted Rouh's red silhouette taking off along the road toward the market, and sent Ali after him. Hearing our tales of woe and looking at Rouh's deathly pale face, the good sheikh wept at the thought that we would soon be parted.

Many a memory has created a bond between the sheikh and us: the times I rode to Amiche and Ourmès with him, the long talks we had and the mystery of our common enterprises . . .

We left shortly before *asr*. We said goodbye in the dunes near Kouïnine. Together with Ali I took the westward road for El Oued, skirting Kouïnine on my left. A handful of women in blue veils were on their way home, bending under the weight of *guerbas* loaded to the brim.

No sooner had we passed Kouïnine than I turned around and took off at a gallop by myself, in hopes of catching up with Slimène. It was too late and I came home by sundown by the deserted road along the Sidi Abdallah cemetery.

~~~~~~~~~~~~

3 February 1901
Is it my destiny to wander on earth for a long time to come?

Where is the haven that would let me rest?

Where are the eyes I can admire?

Where is the breast that would let me rest my head?

~~~~~~~~~~~~

An attempt is made on Isabelle's life in the village of Béhima. The assassin, Abdallah Mohammed ben Lakhdar, attacks her with his sabre; the first blow glances off her head and she receives two more to her arm. The reasons for this assault are shrouded; Isabelle later debates the possibility of an involvement by the French authorities (politically, she is a nuisance in French Africa) or a retaliation of the Qadrya's rival order, the Tidjanya. She describes her assassin's arrest, and in her next journal returns to her experience of the attack itself.

83

9 February 1901

Around five o'clock this afternoon, Abdallah ben Mohammed was put in a prison cell.

I saw him arrive and studied him while he was being searched by soldiers . . . I had a profound feeling of pity for this man, the blind instrument of a destiny whose meaning he does not understand. And seeing that grey silhouette, standing with his head bowed, flanked by the two blue uniforms, I had perhaps the strangest and deepest impression I have ever experienced of *mystery*.

Much as I search my heart for hatred towards this man, I cannot find any. Even less contempt. What I do feel for him is curious: it seems to me that I am close to an abyss, in the presence of a mystery whose last word – or rather whose first word – hasn't yet been spoken, and which would contain the *whole meaning of my life*. As long as I do not know the key to this enigma – and shall I ever know it! God alone knows – I shall not know *who I am*, or what is the reason or explanation of my destiny, one of the most incredible there has been. Yet, it seems to me that I am not meant to disappear without having plumbed the depths of this enigma, from its strange beginnings to the present.

'Madness,' sceptics will say, who like easy solutions and have no patience with mystery. They are wrong, because to see the chasms that life conceals and that three-quarters of the population don't even suspect exist cannot be treated as folly, in the same way that an artist's descriptions of sunset or of a stormy night would seem ridiculous to a man born blind.

If the strangeness of my life were the result of *snobbery*, of a *pose*, yes, then people could say, 'She brought those events on herself', but no! No one has ever lived more from day to day and by chance as I have, and it is very much the events themselves, inexorably linked to one another, which have brought me to where I am and absolutely not me who has created them.

Perhaps the strange side of my nature can be summed up in a single trait: the need to keep searching, come what may, for new events, and flee inertia and stagnation.

JOURNAL THREE

After the attempted assassination, Isabelle is taken to the French Military Hospital in El Oued, to recover from her wounds. She is physically weak and her mood swings between elation, in feeling her life now to be imbued with meaning, and abandonment, in the pit of despair. Slimène is in Batna. She does not keep a chronological journal but goes back and forth in time, interspersing her descriptions of the assault with those of her convalescence.

'In the name of God, the all powerful, the merciful!'

Started at the military hospital in El Oued, February 1901
The long and sleepless winter night seems endless in this deadly silence. It is dark and stifling here in this tiny, narrow hospital ward. The night light on the wall near the window throws a feeble light on the seedy décor: humid walls with a yellow base, two white army beds, a small black table and boards to hold books and bottles. An army blanket hides the window. Not a sound in the barracks' vast courtyard. From time to time my sensitive invalid's ear picks up a long and far-off barking sound, and all is silent once again. Then comes a whisper, the martial sound of soldiers walking with mechanical regularity, a clicking of rifle butts, a brief, impersonal command, with more footsteps going in the direction of the infantry barracks. There has been a changing of the guard at the gate.

Once again, all is silent. In the meantime, I lie here alone, and languish. My injured, shattered head is burning. My whole body is racked with pain. And I cannot find a way to hold my wounded arm. It is giving me a lot of pain and discomfort, and feels terribly heavy; I keep moving it around with my good right arm as best I can. I get no rest whatever I do. I am in pain no matter what I do; a nauseating sort of pain.

Dark and terrible thoughts well up in my sick and feverish mind. My lot looks even more awful and hopeless than it really is. Despair takes hold of me and my chest is gripped with cold fear: 'No, there will be no escaping my assassins.' And they are all, the lot of them, involved in that conspiracy, even the doctor himself.

Suddenly, I see a sheet of white paper on the wall, with rules and regulations written on it in beautiful calligraphy. It is half dark in the room, yet I make an almost desperate effort to read those pedestrian lines. The strain hurts my tired eyes, yet I go on trying to decipher that tight, round, sergeant's script. I fail, and am left feeling hopeless and oppressed.

The details of that fatal day all suddenly come back to me. There, having received a blow to the head, I looked up, and the would-be murderer was stood in front of me, his arms raised high. I could not tell what it was he had in his hands. I then began to moan and sway, my head began to spin and I was overcome with pain and nausea, my thoughts became muddled and suddenly everything grew dim. Then all was dark, and I felt myself sinking. The only thought that crossed my sluggish mind was, *'Death . . . neither fear, nor sorrow.'*

I make another desperate attempt to change my injured arm's position. A dull pain goes through my bone; the severed muscle keeps contracting, so that my fingers are all bent. The wound is deep and has been stitched; it keeps scorching through me. An awful, nameless fear has come over me, and childish tears of frustration are running down my cheeks.

Through the window over the door I can see wan moonlight shine on the building opposite where the autopsy ward is located, with its metal table and boxes full of disinfectants. I may well soon be lying on that hideous table myself. Not that I am afraid of death. I am only frightened of suffering, of long and absurd suffering . . . and also of something dark, undefined, obscure, which seems to surround me, but which I alone can feel . . .

Shiny stars peer down with those impassive, limpid eyes of theirs, as if trying to examine my prison from their inaccessible heavenly heights. The world is one vast, unfathomable mystery and I hang my head in weariness, for I am destitute, alone and ill. I have no source of mercy or of help. There is no limit to the cruelty of men. The only one I cherish and who loves me in return has now been torn from me in a brutal show of Pharisee force.

I am alone, poor, ill . . . I cannot expect any favours or help from anyone . . . Mama is dead, and her + *White Spirit* has left for good the earthly, depraved life that was so alien to her. The old man-philosopher, has also disappeared into the shadows of the grave; the friend and brother is too far away.[29]

And should it be written, should it be my destiny to die right here in this timeless desert, no brotherly hand will come to close my eyes . . . In that last moment on earth, no brotherly lips will utter words of love and consolation.

There is a hint of dawn making its appearance at a premeditatedly slow pace. The western horizon soon takes on the same grey hues as the cupolas just below it. Gloomy, bluish-black clouds hover in the sky, and my room is filling up with the bleak, inhospitable light of morning. How strange a sight over here, where sunlight is so invariably a fiery, royal blaze.

In the distance, the town's innumerable roosters hail each other. From each sound my tutored ear can tell from which part of town the crowing comes, and my worn-out imagination conjures up tableaux from the life I have led here.

Then, all of a sudden, from the side, underneath the infantry barracks' low portico, comes the sound of a trumpet, tentative at first, then loud and piercing. At the same time I hear the creaking sound of the fortress's heavy gates being opened for the day. Then come noises inside the hospital building itself which I have already learned to tell apart: the male nurse in his threadbare Arab slippers, the two corporals wearing their heavy shoes with iron spikes, the sergeant, all these people are starting to come and go. Inside the barracks there are shouts, calls, songs and bursts of laughter. Farther to the east one can hear the clatter of the Spahis' horses being taken to be watered.

Daytime once again, with its people and its noises! Soon that unloquacious and gentle orderly will come limping in with a pot of coffee and a glass. Soon I will recognise the sound of a light tread out on the pavement's cement, a bright red tunic will appear in the doorway, and this whole dreary room will be lit up by that sweet and radiant aura of his, and by those wonderfully soft, luminous brown eyes. Then I will hear the sound of a resonant basso voice with its slight tremor and northern sing-song accent. That is when my soul will feel a measure of serenity again, and my heart will feel less cold.

Written in hospital, 3 February 1901
'The mere name Senegal was enough for him to conjure up that infinite expanse of sand again, those languorous crimson twilights and huge sun setting on the desert . . . He felt curiously attracted to it all, especially the Sahara's edge and impenetrable Moorish frontier.'
  Matelot, Pierre Loti

Isabelle's internal and external worlds are inextricable. Her responses to her surroundings and the landscape here mirror her perception of the meaning of her life and fluctuate as much as her mood.

El Oued, 20 February 1901, 7 a.m.
Went out on horseback for the first time yesterday, on the road to Amiche.

The barracks' grey walls have weighed on me these last few days and I am claustrophobic and oppressed. I feel like a prisoner – yet after yesterday's outing I just want to stay cooped up there, until the day of my departure from the Oued Souf, never to return.

That brief stroll of mine turned into one of the most sad and bitter moments I have ever known. The dunes are still there, and so is the all-grey town, and those deep gardens. Yet the place has lost all of its charm, its magical luminosity . . . the Souf is empty, irrevocably empty, and there is nothing to be done.

The dunes now have a look of desolation, not in that prestigious, mysterious way I used to enjoy, no, they are dead. The gardens all look shabby and the light is grey and dull. As for me, I feel more foreign here than I do in any other place, more lonely too, and I long to flee and leave this place which has become a ghost of what I used to love so much. As long as the aspects of nature all around us *correspond* to our state of mind, we think we see a special beauty there, but from the moment our transient feelings change, everything evaporates and disappears.

I would have liked to leave the Souf with the impression I had before Béhima,[30] to leave overwhelmed by its great and shadowy attraction, a pull that would be fed until the day of my return. How could I have believed in the mysteriousness that I thought I sensed in this country, which was only a reflection of the sad enigma of my own soul? I am condemned to carry my unnameable sorrow, this whole world of thought along with me like this, wherever I go, through the countries and cities of the earth, without ever finding the Icaria of my dreams!

I am as *ignorant* about myself as I am about the outside world. Perhaps that is the only truth.

21 February 1901, noon
Yesterday I went to Guémar for a visit to the good sheikh Sidi El Hussein. It was my heart the other day that was so dark and empty. It was my soul that could not see

the splendour all around. The wind had thrown a shroud of grey dust over all the palm trees and once again played havoc with the dunes between Kouïnine and Tarzout. Those sad little towns – Gara, Teksebet, Kouïnine – all seem so much more desolate and deserted when the great winds of winter blow. The Souf now looks wan under a pallid sky, and the dunes are at their most lacklustre. In the evening, I sometimes hear magic sounds coming from the Messaaba, the infinitely sad music of a tiny Bedouin flute.

In a mere few days' time I shall no longer hear those distant sounds. Hearing the *toubib's* humming this morning suddenly brought me back to my stay in Tunisia – however dead and deeply buried that memory, under so many layers of grey ash, just like my life in the Sahara soon will be. I remember that September night two years ago, when Ali and myself were leaning on our elbows by the little window at La Goulette. On one side I could hear the soft murmur of the placid sea, and on the other, the clear and innocent voice of Sidi Béyène's little Noucha singing that sad Andalusian song: ∪ *My mind is gone, my mind is gone!* Ali's warm and passionate, sonorous voice then took over the wistful refrain, as if in a dream, and all I did was listen . . .

There are moments when I am suddenly reminded of the recent past like that, a period I rarely think of now. Memories of Tunis in particular come to haunt me. Meaningless, forgotten street names come to mind for no good reason.

I went to my house today, and had an awful feeling of emptiness. Going through the door I felt an inward

shudder and thought: 'Rouh' will never enter this place
again . . .'

Never again will we lie in each other's arms, under
the white vault of our small room, sleeping in close
embrace, tightly entwined together, as if we had a strange
premonition of enemy forces in the shadows, seeking
to separate us. Never again will sensual ecstasy unite
the two of us under that roof we have both held so
dear.

Yes, the end has come. In four days' time, I, too, will
head north, a place I would have been too happy never
to see again.

The last of my wistful childish whims is to ask for
burial right here in these white sands gilded at dawn
and dusk by that great and greedy scarlet sun . . .

**Isabelle discharges herself from the hospital too early to
have properly recovered, but eager to embark on the
journey to join Slimène in Batna.**

Departure from El Oued on Monday 25 February 1901, at 1.30 p.m.
26th – Reached Bir-bou-Chama by *maghreb*.

Black sky, grey night, a strong and icy northern wind.
Caravan: *Bach-hamar* Sasi. *Deïras*: Naser and Lakhdar.
Infantrymen: Rezki, Embarek, Salem and El Hadj
Mohammed, from Guémar. Two mental hospital
patients accompanied by a young man (from Algiers).
Hennia, Spahi Zouïzou's[31] mother and her son
Abdallah.

27th – Left at around 7 a.m. Reached Sif-el-Ménédi by
five in the afternoon. Road: trees, plains consisting of

mica and of talc, scrubs; a handful of shotts in the vicinity of the *borj*.

Sif-el-Ménédi: a *borj* set on a very low cliff, scrubby horizon. Well cared for, cultivated garden, salt-water ponds near by. Excellent impression, similar to that of the Oued Rih's salt oases. Lakhdar's dromedary took off in the evening, and the *deïra* went to look for it. I felt exhausted; headache (walked one third of the way). Sat on my bed and thought how nice it would be to live in that *borj* for a while, with the vast maquis for a horizon. Children singing in the garden.

Chegga, Friday 3 March 1901, 9 p.m.
Spent the night at Stah-el-Hamraïa. Spent the evening in the *borj's* main hall, listening to Lakhdar and the camel drivers sing.

Bedded down with Khalifa and infantryman Rezki.

Set out on horseback. Terrain that varied between the salty and the rocky kind. Shrubs of broom with white flowers, Sahara trees, little shrubs with blue flowers. A few shotts, salty soil and yellow sand. Dismounted by the first *guemira*.

A little before the *guemira*, in the maquis on the left, is a wonderfully cool wellspring. Bought some hares from hunters. Set off again on foot. Encountered several caravans. Spotted the tent of a captain in the Engineer Corps at the bottom of a hillside on the left.

Once again we caught sight of shott Meriri, a sea without a horizon, a milky expanse dotted with white islets.

The Nomad

Isabelle is impatient for her sexual reunion with Slimène and fantasizes about their meeting.

Chegga, 1 March 1901
Bedded down in the little room to the left, Khalifa, Rezki and myself. In the large room next door are Hennia and her son. In the other one are the mental hospital patients, their guide and the outcasts. The *deïras* sleep outdoors, with the camel drivers, near the fountain. In the nearby garden flooded with salt water, toads are croaking their melancholy song in the desert's utter silence.

All along the way this afternoon there was the languorous sound of birdsong. A torrid heat all day. I thought lovingly of the way the Sahara has entranced me for life, and what happiness to be back. I had a feeling of boundless and irrepressible energy and of boldness and daring towards fate all day . . . and especially this evening. And yet, another thought haunts me and banishes all possibility of sleep for my weary mind: up in Batna, a rapturous sensuality awaits me, and the thought keeps me tensed in voluptuous expectation . . .

The day after tomorrow, that is to say in two days' time, I can give free reign to a physical desire that is driving me mad this evening, and relive those sensual and abandoned nights of El Oued . . . hold my master in my arms, tight, close to my heart, which is now heavy with the burden of too much unfulfilled love.

This evening, I am aware that I am still young, that life is not so black and empty and that hope is not yet lost. As long as I have the Sahara with its magnificent expanse, I will have a refuge where my tormented soul can go for relief from triviality. To take Rouh' along to distant places, off into the desert, for the pursuit of bold adventures, ineffable dreams, and heady interludes . . .

Isabelle finally reaches Batna. With what little money she has she rents two small rooms. Slimène's almost total confinement to barracks means they can meet only very occasionally, often while still separated by the barrack fence.

Batna, 20 March, 11 o'clock at night
Reached Batna on the 18th at 8.30 p.m.

I would not mind the poverty, which has now become a fact, nor the cloistered existence among Arab women. I might even think it is a blessing to be so totally dependent on Rouh' from now on. What torments me, though, and makes life almost unbearable is the sad and bitter fact that we are apart, and that I can only see him for a fleeting moment now and then. What do I care about the rest, when simply holding him in my arms as I did yesterday and looking into his eyes brings me back to life?

Unprompted and without my being aware of it, the great love of my life, the one I thought would never arrive, has been born!

Batna, Tuesday 26 March, 1 p.m.
Took Souf for a ride today to the foot of the mountain. I let the horse roam freely about the meadow, and myself stretched out beneath a pine tree.

I daydreamed with my gaze upon the great valley, the blue mountains opposite and Batna, city of exile in its slum-like setting. I experienced a sensuous delight at being out of doors in the sun, far from the grey walls of my dreary prison. Everything is turning green again; the trees are in bloom, the sky is blue and countless birds are singing.

High up on those mountains that remind me so much of the Jura or the Salève, the scent of juniper trees and *thujas* was fragrant in the air. The brisk, cool wind rustled softly in the pine trees to resounding echoes from the mountains.

Where is that long-past autumn day when, eyes closed and with a peaceful heart (so much for human nature's utter blindness!), I listened to the strong wind rustle through the tough *djerids* of Debila's palm trees? Where is that Oued Souf of ours, with its white dunes and gardens, and Salah ben Taliba's peaceful house, a stone's throw from the dunes of Sidi Mestour and the silent necropolis that is the Ouled-Ahmed's final resting place? Where is the land of holy *zawyias* and *marabouts*' graves, the harsh, magnificent land that feeds the flames of faith and where we found such bliss? Where has all that gone, and will I ever see it again?

I am in complete destitution. No food, no money, no heating, nothing! The days all come and go, and blend into the past's black void; each new dawn brings us closer to the day of our deliverance, set for 20 February 1902,[32] when real life will truly *begin* for the two of us at last.

Everything is in the hands of God, and nothing happens ∪ *against His will.*

Batna, Friday 12 April 1901, 5 p.m.
These days I go out every morning with my faithful Souf to spend a few hours of quiet in the open space.

At Lambèse I dismount and sit down by the edge of the road, near a field of colza, a vast, brilliantly golden blanket lying at the foot of the dark Ouled-Abdi, for a smoke and time to dream. I hold onto Souf's bridle while he greedily grazes on the green blades of grass he carefully picks out from among the flowers.

Desolate-looking farms dot the long, white ribbon of a road, contrasting with the sharp green of the fields. In the distance to the north, whole fields of flowers palely cover the hillsides in blankets of lilac. The outline of that dreary city, composed of barracks and administrative buildings, is far behind me. My back is turned on it and my gaze is on the countryside in bloom, where the larks are singing and the swallows keep flashing to and fro. I have already come to know this place quite well, and it gives me moments of true bliss and serenity.

The other night I was lying next to Slimène on Khalifa's mat. Through the window I could see the blue sky, a few clouds gilded by the setting sun, the tops of trees that are suddenly green again: all of a sudden, I was reminded of the past, in a flash so keen it left me in tears. The overall landscape is so similar here that memories of *La Villa Neuve* keep haunting me.

Batna, 26 April, 11 o'clock in the evening
I am feeling vaguely depressed tonight, and have for several days now, in a way I cannot define. I feel awfully

lonely without Ouïha,[33] and cannot stand the boredom. Yesterday's storm has left Batna inundated, dark and freezing, and it is full of mud and filthy gutters. My poor Souf is very ill, so that I cannot even go for my rides along the open road, or up to that desolate graveyard where damaged tombs, terrifying windows upon the spectacle of human dust, lie scattered among the fragrant tufts of grey *chih* near a green meadow full of purple flax, white anemones and scarlet poppies in full bloom.

The other day I wandered around among a crowd of Muslims brandishing the flags of ancient religious ceremonies; to the accompaniment of tambours and flutes they prayed for rain, for an extension of their fleeting Algerian spring which already, in its haste to move on, is blending summer flowers with those of spring.

After six long days of only seeing Rouh' for brief and furtive moments by the gate of the hated barracks where he is quartered, he came to see me yesterday . . . I held him in my arms and after the first wild, almost savage embrace, tears ran down our cheeks, and each of us felt a mysterious fear, even though neither of us had said a word or knew why.

I realised yesterday once again how honest, good and beautiful is my Slimène's lovely soul, because of his childish joy about the fact that Augustin was making up with me and so was doing justice to us both.[34] In spite of my past, present and future misfortunes I bless God and my destiny for having brought me to this desert and given me to this man, who is my *only consolation,* my only joy in this world where I am the dispossessed, yet feel the richest, because I have a treasure that is beyond price.

There are times when I am seized with fear, and wonder whether this bliss of mine will be taken from me by death. The only thing is that after him, and the experience I have had with him, I see no point in waiting and hoping. I will go even further: even if I knew that after him I would find another man who would love me just as much, I would not want him, for the simple reason that he would be somebody else and not the man I love so totally, with as much passion as with love and tenderness.

I have often been harsh and unfair, I have been impatient for no good reason, so insane as to hit him, and I am ashamed, because he didn't defend himself and merely smiled at my blind anger. Afterwards I always feel truly miserable and disgusted with myself for the injustice I might have committed.

Increasingly marginalised since the attempt on her life, Isabelle is viewed with suspicion by French authorities. Her movements are being noted and Isabelle realises that she is under surveillance.

This afternoon I went to see the police official who has undoubtedly been detailed by the enemy to spy on me. *He was the first* to come out with the theory that P.[35] was the one who had wanted me killed, and that the murderer was bound to go scot-free. If so, it will be my death sentence wherever I go in the South, the only place I want to live. If the crime committed at Béhima is only slightly punished or not at all, then that will amount to a clear signal to the Tidjanya:[36] 'Go ahead and kill Si Mahmoud, you have nothing to fear.'

Yet God did stay the assassin's hand once, and Abdallah's sabre was deflected. If God wants me to die a martyr, God's will is bound to find me wherever I am. If not, the plots of all those who conspire against me will be their undoing.

I am not afraid of death, but would not want to die in some obscure or pointless way. Having seen death close up, and having felt the brush of its black and icy wings, I know that its proximity means instant renunciation of the things of this world. I also know that my nerves and willpower will hold out in times of great personal ordeals, and that I will never give my enemies the satisfaction of seeing me run in cowardice or fear.

Yet, as I think of the future, there is one thing that does frighten me: the misfortunes that might befall Slimène or Augustin. Faced with those, I have no strength whatsoever. It would be hard to imagine worse poverty than the kind I am up against right now: yet the only reason it worries me is that our debts stand to spell disaster for Slimène. Fortunately, my enemies think I am rich. I was right to throw money out of the window two years ago, and here in Biskra: my reputation for being wealthy is as useful a defence as actual wealth would be.[37] Oh, if those blackguards knew that I am in the direst poverty and that they could ruin us with the least little vexation, they would not hesitate for a moment! What crimes must they have on their conscience . . . Otherwise, why don't they arrest me for espionage or expel me? All because, as P. put it: 'This madwoman could cause us a lot of trouble . . .' I was right to act as if the wretched life I am leading here is a result of indifference and eccentricity: that way, it is not too obvious that I am destitute.

The fact is that I have begun to make a point of going to people's houses to *eat,* for the sole purpose of keeping fit, something that would have been an *anathema* in the old days, like the other thing I have been doing lately, namely going to see *marabouts*, just to beg them for money.

I must have an iron constitution, for my health is holding up contrary to all expectation: those frightening last days in El Oued, the injury, the shock to the nervous system and haemorrhage in Béhima, the hospital, the journey, half of which I made on foot, my poverty here, the cold and poor diet, which mostly consists of bread, none of that has got me down. How long will I be able to hold out?

How in hell can one explain the fact that at home, where I had excellent clothes, warmth and an outstandingly healthy diet, not to mention Mother's idolatrous care, the slightest chill I caught would degenerate into bronchitis; whereas having suffered freezing temperatures at El Oued, and at the hospital as well, having travelled in all kinds of weather, while literally always getting wet feet, going around in thin clothes and torn shoes, I don't even catch a cold? The human body is nothing; the human soul is all.

The only true beauty, in fact, lies in a beautiful soul, for without it, in the eyes of a true aesthete, there is no such thing as physical beauty. Why do I adore Rouh's eyes the way I do? Not for their shape or colour, but for the sweet and guileless radiance of their expression, which is what makes them so astonishingly beautiful.

To me, the soul's supreme achievement would be fanaticism leading *harmoniously*, that is to say, through absolute sincerity, to martyrdom.

In view of the sensitive nature of her continued presence in North Africa after the assassination attempt, 3 May 1901 sees Isabelle receive an order for her expulsion.

Friday 3 May 1901, 9.45 in the morning
Found out last night that I am to be expelled again.

Same day, 3 p.m.
Everything has once again been shattered, broken and destroyed. I shall muster the courage needed to fight the monstrous injustice done to me, and hope to win with God's help.

Yet how can I go off, for God knows how long, and leave Rouh' to whom I am so close? How can I do without him?

Twice more shall we sleep in each other's arms. Twice more shall I see his beloved silhouette in the doorway of the shabby room we have come to cherish. His love and kindness have brought sunshine to this last year's darkest hours; without him, all will be black.

Sunday 5 May, 9 o'clock in the morning
In the midst of all the turmoil I have known these last few days, I am happy to be assured that my sense of beauty and love of nature has lost none of its acuity.

I have reached total destitution and am like a beast at bay being hunted with the single aim of killing, of annihilating it. I am about to be parted from the person who means most to me in life. For years I have known with *certainty* that I would reach this degree of misery. And yet, despite all that, after all the misery I have known and dangers I have faced, I feel that I will not lose heart, I shall not weaken, for two things are intact in me: my religion and my pride, and I'm proud of suffering these uncommon blows, proud of having spilled my blood and having been persecuted for my faith.

Like almost everybody else, I used to think it was absurd to expect that poverty could do anything but stifle one's higher sense of what is good. But there is beauty: on days that I have no way of purchasing material delights, I go to enjoy the gold and scarlet reflections that the sunset casts upon the dunes' white ridges, and I take in the harmony of those sinuous curves and lush hues of spring. Like a vagabond out on the road, I survey the fields of golden colza in bloom, of emerald-green wheat and barley, and opalescent, headily fragrant *chih*.

The grave alone can rob me of such wealth, not man, and who knows, if I am allowed the time it takes to write the odd fragment of a description, it may even survive in the minds of some.

Following her instruction to leave North Africa, Isabelle makes her way to Augustin's house in Marseilles. Slimène remains in Algeria.

Isabelle and Slimène have had Muslim marriage vows witnessed in North Africa, but they must marry under French law or their relationship will continue to be regarded as untenable by French authorities. They experience great difficulties in obtaining official permission to marry. Isabelle discusses the likelihood of her being permitted a permanent return to Algiers.

6 May 1901
Left Batna and arrived at Bône at three in the afternoon. Spent the night of the 6th, the day and night of the 7th and 8th at Koudja ben Abdallah's house.

Written at Bône, 8 May, 6 p.m.
No doubt about it, life without Slimène *will not do*. Everything is bleak and dreary, and time keeps dragging on. Poor Ouïha Kahla! Poor Zizou! When will I ever see him again?

Marseilles, 22 May 1901, 9 p.m.
Wednesday, departure.
Sailed from Bône on Thursday 9 May on the *Berry*, of the Compagnie Générale des Transports Maritimes. Travelled fourth class under the name of Pierre Mouchet, deckhand. Reached Marseilles on Saturday 12th at 3 p.m. Disembarked at Le Môle. Took the tramway to the rue d'Oran.

Tomorrow, when I will have recovered a bit from all the fatigue of the last two days, I shall write down a detailed description of my impressions of Bône, the crossing and first few days in Marseilles. Tonight I only want to go into the psychological aspect of my recent experiences, for having started out in tears and apprehension, things have now suddenly taken a pleasant, because *useful*, turn and brought me such strokes of good luck as, for instance, my amazing encounter with my old friend Sousse Abdel Aziz Agréby, an encounter that may well bring a considerable improvement in Ouïha's predicament and my own; perhaps he will wangle some concession from Algiers; perhaps he will find someone to take Slimène's place in Tunisia? In any event, he will quite probably start reimbursing me for part of what he owes me, little by little . . .

There has been no decree expelling me from the country, which takes care of one terrible threat at least. That means I can go back and join Slimène again as soon as I can find the means to travel, and the Military Court will amply provide me with that before 18 June. In the meantime, I must sit down and do my Russian work and finish it, for which I have now got the time.

The horizon has cleared up a good deal all round. After that strange encounter yesterday with Abdel Aziz, I felt *true friendship* for him: a feeling of great happiness and real emotion. Perhaps he was sent by God to help me through this difficult period in my life!

I think of Slimène, and this may well be the *first* time I do so in *reasonable* terms. Yes, once I am back with him again, I must start behaving differently towards him right away, so that our happiness as a couple is not jeopardised, since marriage must not be based on love alone. No matter how deep and strong, it is not a solid enough foundation. I must go out of my way to show him how devoted I am to him, and must let my kindness outweigh his bitter hardships. I must learn to hold my temper and restrain my selfishness and violence in order not to tax his patience. I must learn the very thing that is hardest for someone of my temperament, namely obedience (which does of course have its limits and must on no account turn into servility), thus making life so much easier for the two of us. To put it in a nutshell, I must change my ways and become easier to live with, which will not be hard to do, what with Slimène's easy good nature and his patience.

Isabelle retrospectively describes her journey to Marseilles, beginning with the departure from Batna, then detailing her voyage by sea. Unable to afford to travel in anything other than the ship's fourth class, she describes having to resort to her old disguise as 'Pierre Mouchet, deckhand', as women are not permitted into the degradation of the fourth class of such vessels. Isabelle reflects upon the irony of her situation, where she must of necessity don the sailor outfit, whereas in Geneva it had been worn as an amusement, and to free her from the social restriction she knew as a woman.

Retrospective notes; copied and completed on 25 May 1901
Left the house in the rue Bugeaud at three in the morning on 6th May. Perfect quiet everywhere, moonlight, dead silence in the streets. Went as far as the entrance to the railway station with Slimène, Labbadi and Khalifa. Sat briefly on a bench Avenue de la Gare. I turned back one last time for another look at that beloved red silhouette as it already lost its contours in the shadows. We parted without too much anguish because we both had the feeling we would soon see each other again.

The countryside between Batna and El Guerrah looked bare and dreary. The *sebhkas*, or lakes, were drowned in white mist. From El Guerrah on, a breathtaking profusion of colours and shades; poppies that looked like so many blood stains on the sombre greenery; snow-white anemones; scarlet gladioli; cornflowers and fields of colza dotting the view.

How I now miss Batna, city of sorrow, love and exile, where my poor good-hearted friend has stayed behind. The same goes for Souf, my valiant and loyal horse, my mute companion on those unforgettable rides through the beloved dunes.

Boarded ship, 9 May at five in the afternoon, when the sky looked pure and luminous.

At Bône, days of boredom and apprehension spent fighting my anxieties about leaving Ouïha to his downfall, about Koudja's passive aggression and pursued by a persistent dark feeling and sense of *unreality* all around me. Bône's magic charm seems to have evaporated and I would not set foot in the place if it were not for the + *White Spirit's* grave!

Once on the *Berry* I sat up front, wretchedly disguised in my Pierre Mouchet sailor outfit, and felt as sad as an emigrant being banished from his native soil. I was suddenly unable to fight back my tears, and had no place to go and hide them. The other passengers all seemed surprised, but did not smile. Felt profound distress at the view of that lively, colourful quay, reddish ramparts, and sacred green hill with its black and sombre cypresses. Felt a sharp twinge of pain at the thought that there, in the early dusk, was Africa vanishing from sight, the ardently beloved soil that harbours both the glorious Sahara and Slimène.

My stay in Bône was so brief and fleeting, and above all so agitated and tormented it might as well have been a nightmare.

Sitting on my bundle by the windlass, I mulled over the hopeless poverty I have come to, the utter destitution that will now be mine. Thought also of the settings I grew up in, the days long past when I was well off and would indulge my taste for dressing as a sailor, of all things.

Made my bed on the spot because it offered a bit of warmth, and dozed off.

Was awakened by a violent storm. Took my rags under the bridge, near the lamp depot. Was told to scram, and wandered around in the torrential rain.

Found shelter near the bow at last, thanks to a kind-hearted sailor, together with two Neapolitans and an old man on his way back from Japan, dressed in a black Arab *kachébia*.

Set off in search of some water. Drank from the reservoir! Had a fairly good night, lying on the floor. Slept all of the next day (10 May) till four in the afternoon.

We were about to hit bad weather; the elderly Neapolitan was feeling seasick. A heavy swell drove me behind the anchor windlass. The ill-tempered ship's boy put me on top of a pile of ropes, on the starboard side.

Violent storm all night long, much heavy tossing and pitching, huge amounts of water taken in by the bow and constantly crashing down on deck with a thunderous roar. An awful night; kept getting splashed, seriously afraid of some calamity. The wind kept wailing and howling, huge waves kept roaring and rumbling . . . a veritable symphony of terror.

Of all the *desperately* lucid thoughts I had that night so full of fever and delirium, I remember one in particular: 'This is the voice of Death bellowing, that's what's carrying on with such a vengeance against the *Berry*, a poor little hull being shaken and tossed about like a mere feather on these hostile waters.' The astonishing thing was that I kept applying meticulous care to find the right words for those disconnected phrases of mine, as if I were trying to write in the midst of all that physical hardship. Seasickness, stomach cramps due to hunger, pain in my right side, freezing temperatures, fatigue and pain in my lower back because of all the clutching I had to do on top of those hard, wet ropes.

All the passengers from the upper deck went down to third class during the night. Was left all by myself, cut off by the constant cataracts thunderously heaving above my head and hitting the deck, which made it impossible for me to pass without running the risk of being crushed.

It was clear and sunny when we docked that afternoon. Quietly took the tramway and dragged my bags all the way on foot.

I am stunned at the lack of news from Slimène. Awoke with a sudden start in the middle of the night, in such a state of anguish I almost went to wake Augustin.

Not a moment's peace all morning, till Slimène's telegram arrived. It gave me the courage needed to bear the latest of my ordeals, the hardest of them all: the fact that we are apart.

A sense of contentment comes over me here in finding, if not affluence, at least the security of a certain comfort that, compared to my own degree of poverty, feels like wealth.

Old, lively memories have come back to me of the time I spent here in November 1899. Listening to the old Marseilles church bells took me back to those sunny days when I would wander around the city, a place I do love dearly but would not want to live in . . . and the Château d'If and Saint-Victor . . . how long ago those sunny autumn days in Provençe seem! But who will give me back the everlasting sunshine of my Souf, with its white *zawyias*, its tranquil homes and grey cupolas, its boundless sandy stretches? And who will give me back Slimène, the friend and lover who is all the family I have on earth?

Isabelle's living in close proximity with Augustin and his wife, Hélène, sees an increasingly tense atmosphere within the household. Having experienced such intimacy as children, Isabelle mourns the dissipation of her relationship with her brother.

Marseilles, 3 June 1901, 9 p.m.
I want to leave as soon as I can, go and join Slimène and never leave him again; do all I can to keep him, for I now know that he is all I have left in this world and that life is not worth living without him. Augustin, to be sure, does all he can for me, but that marriage of his has put a permanent wedge between us, and I can no

longer rely on him the way I used to feel I could. And then there is the *thoughtlessness* of that wife of his, which is to be expected from someone as vulgar as that, but that rules out any life in common with them for me, for I am too lucid about life and things in general.

The only being whom I have ever managed to live with in harmony, and with whom I feel safe, is Slimène. I look forward to the moment of our reunion as to a time of *deliverance*.

As it would in no way affect the impending trial,[38] if the money from Agréby comes in Wednesday's mail, I might leave for Phillippeville on Saturday to be with Slimène a week earlier and cut short the state of anguish I have been in since leaving Batna a whole month ago.

I will have to try to organise my life there in such a way as to make it bearable, especially if we are to stay in Batna for a certain length of time. When I go back after the trial we will only have eight more months of misery ahead of us, at the end of which lies our marriage and freedom. God has always had mercy on us so far and has never let us down, even when things were at their worst.

I find that I have been going through a period of *incubation,* and the odd result is beginning to show: I have a better understanding of people and of things, and my life's outlook is less bleak, although still infinitely sad.

Life is not just a constant struggle against circumstances, but rather *against ourselves*. That's an age-old adage, but most people simply ignore it: hence all the discontent, evil and despair. The mind has *vast* power over itself, and actually exercising that power enhances it even further. Suffering is often the very thing it takes to release that power. Suffering is a good thing because it ennobles. It produces courage and devotion; it creates the capacity for strong feelings and all-encompassing ideas.

I now see that there is one thing I have never understood and never will: *Augustin's character and the kind of life he leads.* Has he become like this, or has he always been this way? He is getting more and more set in his ways and stuck in his present situation, which leaves no room for any intellectual development and strikes me as being more alien and unpalatable all the time.

What, then, lies in store for his child who, I realise with some tenderness and anxiety, looks so much like me?[39] Poor little thing, you will never get to know me, for I shall not be a presence in the house where you will grow up.

Whatever became of the *affinity* there used to be between Augustin's temperament and my own, the one he was always talking about? The closer I look, alas, the less I can find it!

O Slimène, Slimène, stay the way you have been for ten whole months, do not let me down and let me come to you for refuge; you are all I have left!

With time to reflect and as relief from mounting tension within the Marseilles household, Isabelle writes prolifically in this period. She completes two essays, published in Algeria a month later, 'Printemps au désert' and 'El Maghreb', and begins a third, a long essay in Russian, 'Sahara'.

Marseilles, Tuesday 4 June, noon

Had a terrible night doubting everything, especially Rouh'; felt so tormented I thought I might lose my mind.

I blew out my lamp at two o'clock and dozed for a while. Woke up with a start at three o'clock feeling inexplicably frightened, a prelude to the hideous state of despair that lasted until broad daylight.

Irritability, anguish, frayed nerves and a grief so sharp I felt I might go mad; those are the rewards of this latest visit here. And my heart yearns for Slimène more and more every day. In Africa, too, I will know hardship, poverty, boredom and chronic deprivation . . . but I will also have the vast solace of knowing he is there, seeing him and hearing him speak to me, of having someone in whom to confide all my troubles and thoughts, who understands me almost completely, and for whom I represent the same thing he represents for me.

I have a glimmer of hope that there may be some Russian assignment for me, which would improve things considerably. Oh! If Atabek were to send me 20 francs and Agréby 30, I could leave on Friday, go to Batna and put an end to this intolerable state of affairs. Anything, my God, anything to see him again, even for the odd glimpse by the barracks gate, as in the weeks when he was on duty!

On 25 May, Isabelle received a summons to appear in court in Constantine at 6 a.m. on 18 June 1901: the trial of Abdallah Mohammed ben Lakhdar for her attempted murder. The staging of the trial is on the one hand good news, indicating that the French are not attempting a cover-up. However, Isabelle is concerned that it might become a vehicle to strengthen the French position in Algeria – particularly in view of the recent rebel confrontation in Marguerritte – using Abdallah as a scapegoat on whom to pin accusations of Arab anti-European and anti-Christian revolutionary action. It is with this in mind that she decides to make her position clear, in an open letter to the Algiers paper, *Dépêche Algérienne*, stating that as a known Muslim convert, she was not the target of anti-Christian fanaticism.

Marseilles, Friday 7 June 1901
May 6, publication of my letter concerning the Béhima episode in the *Dépêche Algérienne*.

Sent letter of rectification on the 7th.

Sir,

On June 18th next, a native by the name of Abdallah Mohammed ben Lakhdar, from the village of Béhima near El Oued (district of Touggourt), will appear before the Military Court at Constantine for trial. He stands accused of murder, or rather of attempted murder, and his guilt is an established fact. I myself was the victim of his deed, which almost cost me my life.

I have been quite surprised to find no mention of the affair in the Algerian press, despite the fact that it is one of the strangest and most mysterious cases ever to have been tried in an Algerian court. I can only suppose that the press has been left in the dark about the facts. I believe that for the sake of justice and truth the public ought to learn a number of details before it comes to trial. I would be most obliged if you would be so kind as to publish this letter under my name. The responsibility for its contents is entirely mine.

I should like to preface my story with a few facts, in order to clarify the tale that follows.

The investigating magistrates have repeatedly expressed their surprise at hearing me describe myself not only as a Muslim but also an initiate of the Qadrya sect;and they have not known what to make of my going about dressed as an Arab, sometimes as a man, and at other times as a woman, according to the needs of my essentially nomadic life.

In order that I should not be thought of as someone affecting Islamism for show, or assuming a religious label for some ulterior motive, I wish to state unequivocally that I have not been baptised and have never been a Christian; that although a Russian subject, I have been a Muslim for a very long time. My mother, who belonged to the Russian aristocracy, died in Bône in 1897, after having become a Muslim, and now lies buried in the Arab cemetery there.

Consequently, I have no reason to convert to Islam, nor to play-act in any way, something that my fellow-believers in Algeria have understood perfectly, to the extent that Sheikh Si Mohammed El Hussein, brother of the naïb of the Ouargla brotherhood, Si Muhammad Taïeb, has agreed without reservation to initiate me into the sect. The reason for my explaining all this is to nip in the bud any suggestion that the motive for Abdallah's attempt on my life lies in a fanatical hatred against everything Christian, for I am not a Christian and all the Souafas know it, Abdallah included!

What follows is a description of the attempt made on my life, at three in the afternoon on 29th January. It took place in the house of a certain Si Brahim ben Larbi, a landlord in the village of Béhima, 14 kilometres to the north of El Oued along the road to the Tunisian Djerid.

I had visited El Oued at the time of my first journey into the Constantine part of the Sahara, in the summer of 1899, and had a vivid memory of the area's immaculate white dunes, lush gardens and shady palm groves. In August 1900, I went to live there for an indefinite period of time. That was where I was initiated into the Qadrya brotherhood, and became a regular visitor to the three zawyias *located near El Oued, having won the friendship of the three sheikhs, sons of Sidi Brahim and brothers of the late* naïb *of Ouargla. In January I accompanied one of them, El Lachmi, to the village of Béhima. He was on his way to Nefta in Tunisia with a group of* khouans *for a* ziara *at the grave of his father, Sidi Brahim. For reasons of my own I could not go as far as Nefta, but accompanied the sheikh to Béhima where the pilgrims were to spend the night. I expected to return to El Oued that same evening with my manservant, a Sufi who had followed me on foot. We entered the house of the man named Ben Larbi, and the* marabout *withdrew to another room for the afternoon prayer. I myself stayed in a large hall giving onto an antechamber that led into the public square, where there was a dense crowd and where my servant was looking after my horse. There were five or six Arab figures of note, both from the village and the surrounding area, most of them Bhamania* khouans.

I was sitting between two of them, the owner of the house and a young tradesman from Guémar, Ahmed ben Belkassem. The latter had asked me to translate three telegrams for him, one of which was badly written and gave me a great deal of trouble. My head was bent in concentration, and the hood of my burnous *covered my turban, so that I could not see what was going on in front of me. I suddenly felt a violent blow to my head, followed by two more to my left arm. I looked up and saw a badly dressed man, obviously a stranger to the house, brandishing a weapon above my head, which I took to be a truncheon. I leapt up and ran to the opposite wall to try to seize El Lachmi's sword, which was hanging there. But the first blow had hit the crown of my head and dazed me, and I fell onto a travelling trunk, aware of an acute pain in my left arm.*

A young Qadrya mokaddem *named Si Muhammad ben Bou Bekr and a servant of Sidi Lachmi's named Saad disarmed the assassin, but he managed to free himself. When I saw him coming toward me, I stood up and tried to grab the sabre again, but could not because my head was spinning and the pain in my arm was too sharp. The man ran out into the crowd, shouting: 'I am going to find a gun to finish her off.' Saad then showed me a sword whose blade was dripping with blood, and said: 'This is what the cur wounded you with!'*

Alerted by the commotion, the marabout *came running in, and he was immediately given the name of the assassin by the people who had recognised him. He sent for Béhima's independent sheikh who, like the assassin, belongs to the Tidjanya brotherhood.*[40] *It is common knowledge that the latter are the Qadrya's staunchest adversaries in the desert. The sheikh in question stubbornly resisted the* marabout's *request with various ploys, telling him that the murderer was a* sherif, *etc. etc. The* marabout *publicly threatened to tax him with complicity in the eyes of the Arab Bureau, and insisted that the assassin be arrested on the spot and taken away. The sheikh finally did so, but with very bad grace.*

The culprit was taken into the same room where I had been put down on a mattress. He first pretended to be mad, but was caught out by his own fellow citizens who knew him to be a calm, reasonable and sober man. He then said God had sent him to kill me. I was fully conscious and knew that I had no idea who the man was. I began to interrogate him myself and he said he did not know me either, had never set eyes on me but had come to kill me nevertheless. He said that if he were set free, he would attempt it all again. When I asked him what he had against me, he replied: 'Nothing, you have done me no wrong, I don't know you, but I must kill you.' When the marabout asked him whether he knew that I was a Muslim, he said he did.

His father, when summoned, said they were Tidjanyas. The marabout forced the local sheikh to inform the Arab Bureau, and asked both for an officer to come and fetch the culprit and start an investigation, and for a medical officer for me.

The investigating officer, a lieutenant from the Arab Bureau, and the doctor showed up by eleven o'clock. The doctor found my head wound and the injury to my left wrist to be superficial; I owed my life to sheer luck: a laundry-line just above my head had cushioned the first blow, which would otherwise certainly have been fatal. My left elbow, however, had been cut to the outside bone; both the muscle and the bone had been severely slashed. I had lost so much blood in six hours that I was very weak, and I had to be kept in Béhima for the night.

The next day I was taken by stretcher to the military hospital at El Oued, where I remained till February 26th. Despite Dr Taste's efforts, I left the hospital a cripple for life, unable to use my arm at all for anything strenuous.[41]

At the time of my first journey, I had run into difficulties with the Arab Bureau at Touggourt, which oversees the one at El Oued, difficulties that were due solely to the suspicious attitude of the Touggourt Bureau. The head of the Arab Bureau at El Oued, its officers, those at the garrison and the army *doctor have all been extremely good to me and I should like to express my thanks to them publicly.*

The investigation showed that for five days before committing his crime, Abdallah had tried to buy firearms, but had been unable to find any. The day we arrived in Béhima, he had transferred his family – the poor devil has young children – and his belongings to the house of his father, where he had not lived for six years. Although both father and son were prominent Tidjanyas, they had both suddenly withdrawn from their brotherhood; the father told me he was a Qadrya, and the son told the investigating magistrate he was a member of the Mouley-Taïeb brotherhood. The police officer, Lieutenant Guillot, established that Abdallah was lying.

A few days before I left El Oued there was a rumour among the native population that shortly before the crime, Abdallah, who had been riddled with debts, had gone to Guémar (centre for the Tidjanya) and that upon his return he had settled his debts and even bought a palm grove. At about the same time, Abdallah's father went to Sidi Lachmi's zawyia, and, before witnesses, told him that his son had been paid to attack me, but, since he did not know himself who the instigators were, he was seeking permission to see his son in the presence of an official in order to get him to make a full confession. The marabout *advised him to go to the Arab Bureau. The old man also asked one of my servants if he could speak to me, and, telling me: 'This crime did not start with us'; added that he was anxious to see his son in order to persuade him to come clean. Those are the facts.*

Now, it is clear that Abdallah was not motivated by any hatred of Christians, but that he was pushed into it and acting on behalf of others, and then that his crime was premeditated. I told the investigating authorities that, in my view, the attempted murder can best be explained by the hatred of the Tidjanya for the Qadrya, [42] *and that the reason for the Tidjanya kaba or khouans wanting to do away with me was that they knew their enemies loved me – witness the khouans' grief at hearing about the crime. As I passed through the villages around El Oued on a stretcher on my way to the hospital, the inhabitants, men and women alike, all came to the road to shout and wail the way they do for funerals.*

I trust the Military Court at Constantine will not be content merely to convict and sentence Abdallah ben Mohammed and let it go at that, but will also try to throw light on this nebulous affair.

It seems to me that Abdallah was only an instrument in other hands and his conviction will not satisfy me, nor, for that matter, anyone who cares for truth and justice. It is not Abdallah whom I would like to see in the dock, but rather those who incited him, that is, the real culprits, whoever they may be.

I trust, Sir, that you will not refuse to publish this letter in your worthy newspaper, for I believe it to be of some interest. From the political, if not a social point of view, the Algerian Tell is not all that different from the other French provinces; however, the same cannot be said of the Sahara, where life is very different indeed, to a degree that people in France can hardly begin to imagine.

ISABELLE EBERHARDT

Isabelle writes to the editor of *Dépêche Algérienne*, in thanks for the publication of her previous letter. She refers to her position regarding colonialism and describes her close relationship with the Arab community. Her correspondence again appears in the paper.

Marseilles, 7 June 1901

Sir,

I should like to thank you most sincerely for having published my long letter dated May 29th. I should add that I could hardly have expected less from a newspaper with your reputation for impartiality: the Dépêche Algérienne *has always shown considerable moderation, compared with the excesses that have unfortunately become standard policy for other Algerian publications. It seems to me, however, that as the question of foreigners residing in Algeria is such a burning topic at the moment, I ought to expand upon my earlier letter for those who have taken the trouble to read it.*

You have credited me with an honour I do not deserve in the least – that is, your assertion that I have a certain degree of religious influence on the native population in the district of Touggourt. In actual fact I have never played, nor tried to play, any political or religious role, for I feel I have neither the right nor the requisite competence to meddle with anything as serious and complex as religious matters in a country of this sort.

At the time that I set off for Touggourt in 1899, I felt it was my duty to go and see Lieutenant Colonel Tridel, who was in charge of the district of Biskra, and inform him of my departure. This officer gave me a most cordial reception and, with military forthrightness, asked me point-blank whether I was an English Methodist missionary. I showed him my papers, which are all in order and which leave no doubt about the fact that I am Russian and have permission from the imperial authorities to live abroad. I also gave Lt. Col. Tridel my opinions on the subject of English missions in Algeria, and I explained that I abhorred all kinds of proselytism and above all hypocrisy, which is the feature of the English character, as unappealing to us Russians as it is to the French.

The officer I found to be in charge of the Arab Bureau in Touggourt in the absence of the commanding officer was a captain by the name of De Susbielle, a strange man of an odd turn of mind. Once again I had to establish that I was no English Miss in Arab disguise, but a Russian writer. One would think that if there is one country where a Russian ought to be able to live without being suspected of dubious intentions, that country should be France!

The officer in charge of the El Oued Bureau, Captain Cauvet, saw for himself over a six-month period that there was nothing to be held against me, apart from my eccentricity and a lifestyle that is perhaps a bit unexpected for a young girl like myself, but quite innocuous just the same. It did not occur to him that my preferring a burnous to a skirt, and dunes to a domestic hearth could present any danger to the public security in the Annexe.

As I have stated in my earlier letter, both the Souafas belonging to Sidi Abdel Kader's brotherhood and those of other ones friendly to it have all let me know how sorry they were to hear there had been an attempt on my life. The reason these good people all had a certain affection for me is that I had helped them as best I could and had used what little medical knowledge I had to treat the ophthalmia, conjuctivitis and other complaints that are endemic to the area. I had attempted to be of some help in my vicinity, and that was the extent of my role in El Oued.

Hardly anyone in this world is without a passion or mania of some sort. To take as an example my own gender, there are women who will do anything for beautiful clothes, while there are others who grow old and grey poring over books to earn degrees and status. As for myself, all I want is a good horse as a faithful and dumb companion to a solitary and contemplative life, and a few servants barely more complicated than my mount, and to live in peace, as far away as possible from the agitation of civilised life, where I feel so deeply out of place.

How can it harm anyone, if I prefer the undulating misty horizons of the dunes to the boulevards?

No, Monsieur le Directeur, I am not a politician, nor am I an agent of any particular party, because to me they are all equally wrong in their exertions. I am only an eccentric, a dreamer anxious to live a free and nomadic life, far away from the civilised world, in order to try to say afterwards what she has seen and perhaps to communicate to some people the charm, the melancholy and the thrill which I have felt in the face of the sad splendours of the Sahara . . . That's all.

It is of course true that in the summer of 1899 it was unusually hot in the Sahara, and that mirages will distort many a perspective and account for many an error!

I. E.

At long last I am almost certain of being able to leave on Friday. That means being here for only another seven days. I am sure that Augustin will do all he can to procure me the money I need.

Poor Augustin! However enigmatic he may seem, he is good to me and nothing in this world will ever succeed in killing the deep and everlasting affection I feel for him. Oh! What a pity that marriage of his makes it impossible for him to come and join Slimène and myself for a truly wonderful life! It is best, though, for everyone concerned that I leave, and at the end of this week I shall have the inexpressible joy of seeing Slimène

again, of holding him in my arms and ∪ *if Allah is willing,
never leaving him again.*

Spent the better part of last night feeling abominably
ill: dizziness and awful headache.

Once in Batna, I will have to do my best to save every
penny I can, to be reimbursed as much money as
possible and above all, to work in Russian: that way lies
the only chance I have of earning an income fairly soon.
That will not be too trying, provided my health holds
out after the awful shocks it has had. To work so that I
can stay with Ouïha, that is my duty. He will find a
way to make it up to me for the hard work I will do.

This evening I wrote a letter for Ahmed Cherif and
as I was doing so, I remembered the autumn of 1899.
What became of the life of mystery and adventure I then
led in the Sahel's vast olive groves?[43] How very strange
the names I knew so well now sound to me: Monastir,
Sousse, Moknine, Esshyada, Ksasr, Ibellal, Sidi N'eidja,
Beni-Hassane, Anura, Chrahel, Melloul, Grat-Zuizoura,
Hadjedj . . . What of that incomparable country, an African
version of Palestine with its lush, green meadows and
little white villages lying reflected in the blue water of
its tranquil bays? And what of Sousse, with its Moorish
white ramparts and revolving beacon, and of Monastir,
where waves never cease to roar and break upon the
reefs?

Under the terms of her exclusion from North Africa,
Isabelle leaves France for Algeria on 13 June, instructed
of her attendance at Abdallah's trial in Constantine. She
returns to Marseilles less than a week later, on 20 June.

Arrived in Constantine on Saturday 15th at ten past nine. Went to the Café Zouaouï. Set out with Hamou the porter to look for Ben-Chakar. Located him around noon. In the evening, Café Sidi Ksouma. Sunday 16th, six o'clock train, met Ouïha. Night at Hôtel Metropole, rue Basse-Damrémont. Monday 17th, arrival of Sidi Lachmi.

The 18th, 6 a.m. – the trial. Came out at eleven. Thursday 20th, left for Phillipesville at 6.30. Arrived there at 9.35. Night at Hôtel Louvre.

Thursday 4 July 1901, noon
Zouïzou has left on the *Touareg*. Day of gloom, anguish and despair. When will we see each other again?

Isabelle retrospectively describes her journey to Constantine, her joy at returning to Africa, the emotion with which she is greeted by her Arab friends and her attendance at Abdallah's trial.

Travelling by sea on the *Félix-Touache*, Isabelle again disguised herself as a boy and travelled in fourth class. She met an ex-convict, Amara, who told her he had just come out of prison for killing a man, an act of revenge for the theft of his horse.

Marseilles, 5 July 1901
The evening of my arrival at Philippeville on the *Félix-Touache,* I had that feeling of well-being, of *rejuvenation* I always get when reaching the blessed coast of my African fatherland, a feeling so at odds with the way I react every time I reach Marseilles. My arrivals here are as depressing as the ones over there are cheerful!

With the Ouled-Aly convict Amara, Sétif and Borj-ben-Aréidj, I went up to the deserted deck and settled on the starboard side, in the silence of the harbour's chilly night. I descended alone to the steerage at three o'clock: matches wet, so no way to light a lamp. Got dressed groping about in the dark. Went back on deck, woke up Amara.

Mountains, fertile slopes and plains all the way to Constantine. Amara thrilled like a child at the sight of fields, tents and herds. Islamic soil, fatherland of nomads: Constantine's magnificent rocks appeared on the horizon at last.

We disembarked at the station. I went into the Café Zouaouï at last, feeling embarrassed with my *roumi's* cap on. Stayed for quite a while and talked with the owner, an inveterate smoker of *kef*. I then set out with *hamel* Hantou to look for Muhammad ben Chakar. Steep and narrow winding streets, squares on a slope, intricate crossroads, silent, shady corners, the immaculate, ornately carved porchways of old mosques, covered bazaars – it all went to my head the way ancient Arab décors always do.

We wandered around and asked . . . at long last we did discover Ben Chakar's abode: right at the top of an alleyway's steps, a cul-de-sac with a floor made of wooden beams above it at barely six feet above the ground, the floor of an *ali* or dark sort of den where one had to walk bent over for four or five yards. Suddenly we came upon a Moorish interior, bluish-white in colour just like the ones at Bône.

Muhammad ben Chakar's brother smokes *chira* as well as *kef*; he sometimes works as a porter, sometimes as a café-owner or a fritter-vendor, very congenial. His wife was pleasant, too, bright and mannish.

In the afternoon Ben Chakar and I set off for the Gorges du Rhummel, vertiginous chasms with frail-looking bridges hung across them, often in the shadows, and subterranean stairways and endless labyrinths. Met a few Constantinian craftsmen. Went to the Jewish baths, had great fun splashing about like overgrown children. Came back by the road above the abyss, along the shore opposite the city.

Went to Sidi Ksouma's café in the evening, and had the distinct feeling that *Zouïzou was in Constantine.* Sat in a corner in my Arab garb, which made me feel at ease, and listened to the singing and beating of the tambourine until quite late. Feast of Beldia: pale, distinguished faces, empty of expression, eyes half-closed . . .

Had a bad night, due to anxiety and *fleas* . . .

Sunday 16 June – Went to the station in vain. Went for a stroll to Bab-el-Oued with young Salah. Met the *bach-adel* of Biskra.

By evening, still no news from Zouïzou; in desperation I went to the station with Elhadj at 6.35 p.m. to meet the train from Philippeville. Despondent, we sat down on a stone and waited. Elhadj spotted Ouïha at last, in native civilian garb. Went for supper at Ben Chakar's, dressed as a Moorish woman, and after that went to the Hôtel Metropole, far away in the rue Basse-Damrémont. A night of joy, bliss, tenderness and peace.

Early next morning, Monday 17th, went to the station to meet Sidi Lachmi. Spotted the tall figures of the Souafa witnesses in front of the station: Hama Nine,

Mohammad ben Bou Bekr and Brahim ben Larbi. Felt terribly moved at the sight of those *countrymen* of mine, who spoke with their local accent and all embraced me with tears in their eyes. Went out onto the platform with the group of Souafas to welcome our beloved Grand Sheikh,[44] who smiled to see me.

Went on an endless search for a hotel with Hama Nine. Hostile refusals everywhere. Found temporary accommodation at the Metropole at last. Felt very comforted in being reunited with the sheikh, Bechir and all the others.

Problems at the hotel. Transfer of the nomads' *zawyia* to the Hôtel Ben Chimou, on the Marché du Chameau, near the theatre, so spent the night in some second-floor Jewish room, 6 rue Sidi Lakhdar.

The trial of Abdallah Mohammed ben Lakhdar took place on 18 June. Although unable to afford to buy European clothes, Isabelle prudently chose to wear feminine Arab garments, rather than dress in her usual attire of her male alter-ego, Si Mahmoud Essadi.

On Tuesday 18th, we arrived at the courthouse at 6.30 a.m. The guard brought me a cup of coffee in the witnesses' waiting room where I was by myself, an object of curiosity for the growing crowd of passers-by, officers, and ladies. I saw Abdallah, in handcuffs, flanked by an escort of *zouaves*.

Captain Martin, the Government Commissioner, came to shake my hand, as did his sister. At seven o'clock, the bailiff came to fetch me. The courtroom was packed. I did not feel too intimidated, and sat down next to Sidi Lachmi. Our two chairs faced the double row of witnesses on their benches. Not exactly run of the mill, those witnesses in their box: tanned, expressive faces, garbed in clothes either white or dark, with a single contrasting *burnous* the colour of blood, the red one worn by that traitor Muhammad ben Abderrahmane, sheikh of Béhima. Sidi Lachmi was dressed in green and white.

The court: a group of uniforms, medal-bedecked torsos sitting stiffly and inscrutably. Arms were presented; the presiding judge timidly opened the trial with a frail and quavering voice. The court clerk read the charges and called out the witnesses' names, starting with myself. We then were made to file out of the room one by one.

In the witnesses' room, Captain Gabrielli and the young lieutenant who is his secretary came to shake my hand. We talked for quite a while.

Someone came to fetch me. The judge was about to call the witnesses. The bailiff told me to stand in front of the presiding judge, and I was made to repeat the oath.

Still shy, the judge kept stammering as he questioned me from his notes. It did not take long. The interpreter called Abdallah and asked him: 'Have you anything to say to so-and-so?'

'No,' was Abdallah's firm and simple reply, and despite everything that had been said, 'all I have to say is that I ask her to forgive me.'

I returned to my seat. Sidi Lachmi came in and testified in a simple and unruffled way. After that came the sheikh, who was followed by Ben Bou Bekr, Brahim ben Larbi, and then the assassin's father, simpering as usual.

After a five-minute recess we heard Captain Martin's speech for the prosecution which, although based on a theory that must be erroneous, was a vibrant plea in favour of the Qadrya and myself. The defence lawyer, who exasperated me, spoke next. A reply from Captain Martin, and further words from the lawyer. The court withdrew. The room was buzzing with voices.

Abdallah Mohammed ben Lakhdar was found guilty of attempted premeditated murder and sentenced to life's hard labour. Appalled by the severity of the sentence, Isabelle composed the following statement, reiterating her determination to see a fair carriage of justice. She then wrote to Abdallah and lodged an appeal on his behalf. His sentence was reduced to ten years in prison.

At the trial, Isabelle was served a formal expulsion order, a decree barring her from Algeria.

ISABELLE'S STATEMENT

As I have already pointed out, both to the investigating authorities and in my two letters to the Dépêche Algérienne, *I am firmly convinced, and always will be, that Abdallah was the instrument of people who had an interest – real or imagined – in getting rid of me. It is obvious that if he was indeed bribed to kill me, which is what he told his father at the time of his arrest, he could not expect to reap any benefits from his deed, for he committed it in a house full of people whom he knew to be on friendly terms with me, and he knew he would be arrested. It is therefore clear that Abdallah is mentally unbalanced. He has said he is sorry and even asked me for forgiveness during* the trial. I think that today's verdict is out of all proportion, and wish to state that I deplore its severity. Abdallah has a wife and children. I am a woman and can only grieve with all my heart for his widow and her orphans. As for Abdallah himself, I feel only the deepest pity for him.

At the end of this morning's trial, I have had the painful surprise of learning that the Governor General has issued a decree expelling me from the country. According to the terms of the decree, I am being banned from all Algerian territory, whether under civilian or military control. I can only wonder about the rationale for this measure. I am a Russian and can in all good conscience say that I have done nothing to deserve it. I have never participated in nor been aware of any anti-French action, either in the Sahara or in the Tell. On the contrary, I have gone out of my way to defend the late naïb of Ouargla, Sidi Muhammad Taïeb – who died a hero's death fighting alongside the French – against the accusations made by a handful of Muslims who have argued that the naïb had betrayed Islam by installing the French at In Salah. Wherever I have been, I have always spoken favourably of France to the native people, for it is my adopted country. That being so, why am I being expelled? Not only does this measure offend my Russian sensibilities, it also puts me in a particularly painful situation as it will separate me from my fiancé for months to come; he is a non-commissioned officer at the Batna garrison, and is therefore not free to leave. I could perhaps have understood my being banned from territories under military control, in order to avoid my falling victim to revenge from Abdallah's tribe. I have no intention of returning to the South, however. All I ask is to be allowed to live in Batna and marry the man who was at my side during my ordeal and is my only source of moral support. That is all . . .

Isabelle explores her sense of destiny, her attraction to the philosophy of Islamic resignation of the self to God's will and intimates her belief in a mystical calling. She realises that she would be ridiculed should she broadcast her ideas, and is aware of the difficulties of explaining these phenomena and her interpretations, even in these private papers.

Marseilles, 8 July, 2 p.m.
I am going through a period of composure, both physical and emotional, of intellectual awakening and hope *without frenzy,* and time is going by fairly fast, which is the main thing just now.

Since that notorious trial in Constantine, I have felt a strong literary urge coming to the fore. My gift for writing is really coming to life these days. I used to have to wait, sometimes for months, for the right moods to write in. Now, I can write more or less whenever I want. I think I have reached a point where the potential I had been aware of all along has now begun to blossom.

As for my religious feelings, my faith is now truly genuine, and I no longer need to make the slightest effort. Before I go to sleep at night, I look deep down into my conscience, and never fail to find the blissful peace there that comes from the mysterious knowledge that will henceforth be my strength.

For me, life acquired a meaning from the instant I understood that our journey down here is a steady process of human development towards another life: it is natural, therefore, that there is an imperative to strive for moral and intellectual perfection – which would be inappropriate, because useless, without an after-life.

I must apply myself to my intellectual progress and find an outlet for the two articles I sent off to Angellini this afternoon, 'Printemps au désert' and 'El Maghreb'. I must pursue my reading, certain books including and in the vein of Bourget's *Essais de psychologie contemporaine*. And as soon as I am settled in, I must reread the *Journal des Goncourts* – it had such a good effect on me last year and will be good for me as a writer – as well as other works likely to do the same for my intellect.

But the other question which preoccupies me is of quite a different order, and one which I could only talk through with Slimène, who is *the only person who would understand* and acknowledge it; and that is the *maraboutic* question,[45] a thought that spontaneously came to me the evening Abdallah was transferred from the civil prison to his cell. And Slimène had thought of it too, no doubt from an intuition born from our great spiritual affinity! . . . It seems to me that with willpower, I will have no trouble reaching a mysterious goal like that; one that would offer infinite satisfaction and would open up unforeseen possibilities. ∪ *Lead us in the straight and narrow path,* and I do believe that, for me, this is the path.

God has sown some fertile seeds in my soul: my faith; an extreme disinterestedness towards the *things* of this world; and an infinite love and concern for everything that suffers. This forgiveness of evil is an expression of my unlimited devotion to the cause of Islam, which is the most beautiful of all because it is the cause of truth . . . Oh, the long hours I used to spend in the shadows and shade of the woods, the sleepless nights spent gazing at the extraordinary world of the stars . . . wasn't I already on the direct path to religious mysticism?

A different choice in life-long companion would certainly have thwarted the necessary progress toward a future of that sort. Slimène will follow me wherever I go, and of all the men I have known, he is the *only true* Muslim, for he *loves* Islam with all his heart and is not content with paying mere lip service.

If a scholar or a psychologist or a writer were to read these words they would be sure to exclaim: 'She's one step away from madness!' Well, if ever the flame of intelligence has burned within me, it is now, and what is more, I know that I am only on the threshold of a whole *new life*.

Maître Laffont[46] unwittingly hit upon a truth when he said that I ought to be more grateful to Abdallah. That I am, yes, and what is more, I *sincerely love Abdallah,* for he *was* the heavenly emissary he said he was. It is likely that others were behind his deed, people who are the true culprits; he himself, however, must have been sent by God, for ever since that fateful day in Béhima I have felt my soul move into a whole new phase in its earthly existence. In some mysterious way, Abdallah's life-long suffering will no doubt pay for the redemption of another's life.

Abdallah will go to the farthest corner of the earth on the other side of the planet. What he has wrought did fall on fertile soil, has begun to germinate and will one day emerge from the shadows where I keep it hidden. That is my secret, one I must not reveal or talk about, except with the one man who discovered it all by himself one day, who never desecrates the sanctuary of my soul with mocking laughter.

All those who in their blindness think they have eyes to see may condescendingly shrug or smile in the presence of the couple that we form. It is based on something else, on sentiments and aims that have nothing in common with those marriages of theirs, motivated as they are by base venality, ambition and infantile lust. Ours is a love *beyond* their understanding.

Permission for Slimène's permutation to a Marseilles regiment is imminent and Isabelle anticipates their marriage. Although in her eyes their love and pledged Muslim vows have already bound them together, she looks forward to a public assertion of their relationship.

Thursday 11 July 1901, 9 in the evening
I am not in the mood right now to go on with my description of the trial. For the moment, other thoughts and other memories have come to haunt me.

Felt bored and ill at ease last night, just like the day before. Anxiety this morning and much physical tension in the absence of any letter from Ouïha.

Went down to the Cours du Chapitre around 9.30 this morning to post a letter to Zouïzou. In the afternoon, I started on my Russian assignment without much conviction. Had a good letter at last by three o'clock. The question of Zouïzou's replacement has *definitely* been settled and his return is now only a matter of days; time will pass by very quickly, now that I *know* he is coming.

I think he should be able to get here by the morning of the 23rd. That day will be the start of a whole new life. Of course, there will still be days of gloom and moments of distress, for otherwise life would not be what it is. There are times when suffering has its uses. Yet I have the feeling that the age of separations is drawing to a close at last.

What a sigh of relief we will heave, my God, after our visit to City Hall, which will bind us to each other at long last and mean that others are *obliged* to treat us as a couple. God treated us that way and gave us his blessing a long time ago, in the form of love. Now men will soon lose the right to part us!

In a few days' time it will be a year since I last arrived in the Sahara. Of that time I curse nothing, not a single episode, except for my banishment, and even that, why curse it, after all? How many years did I spend in useless, sterile and irrelevant recriminations? Who knows? It may be that when I saw death so close up and almost crossed its threshold, it was the truth I saw at last, and perhaps have I now understood that there is a *meaning,* an inner logic and a goal to this paltry life of ours, no matter how few people love and appreciate it! For the fact is that few people *love* life, and I do not mean in the unconscious way of animals, but for its *true,* magnificent splendour. Inept pseudo-philosophers all, saddled as they are with unhealthy innards and a sickly liver, who keep roaring their blasphemous insults!

Memories of this time last year are haunting me . . . Geneva, times of anguish and of joy in my Russian way of life out there; the moment of my sailing for the beloved, fateful land of Barbary from whence I have now been banned, but where I shall soon be able to return with my head held high ∪ *if it pleases Allah!*, and white Algiers, where I used to lead a double life, an unorthodox and heady one among people who had respect and even admiration for me, even though they knew nothing about me, not even what my gender was! Strange, intoxicating rides with Mokhtar, *kef*-smoking sessions . . . the way we sang sad Algerian cantilenas on our strolls along the quays . . . the white *zawyia* of Sidi Abd-el Rahman ben Koubrine, miniature city of one's dreams basking in the golden sunset above the fragrant Jardin Marengo . . . the ecstasy felt during the *icha* prayer hour in the Jadid mosque. . . Oued Rir with its magic spell and unforgettable splendour . . . Touggourt asleep in its desert of salt, with its mirror image in the sluggish waters of its shott . . . and farther on, the familiar road leading to the goal of that long journey, the splendid outline of the one and only City, the city of my choice, predestined El Oued!

'Man cannot flee his destiny!'

Monday 15 July 1901, 11 in the morning
Felt very odd last night, for no discernible reason: a memory of my arrival at Sousse, two years ago . . . and the desire to travel alone to some uncharted place in Africa, where no one knows me, the way no one did when I came to Algiers last year . . . but with adequate means this time.

Generally speaking, I feel a desire for mental *isolation,* although not for long, for I still miss Slimène. I would like to have a month all to myself before his return, and the necessary funds for a leisurely voyage by myself

. . . I know I would come back with very valuable, pertinent observations. Yet this is a period in which my outlook is lucid and level-headed, and above all it is a period of work. The hope that a better life is just around the corner has, of course, a good deal to do with my present frame of mind.

It will soon be six months since that fateful episode at Béhima. Even though I did not realise it then, that day was the beginning of another period of incubation, the sort I have experienced all my life, for quite clearly my intellectual development has always been achieved by *fits and starts,* so to speak: periods of restlessness, discontent and uncertainty have always been followed by the emergence of a better version of myself. A subject to be analysed, and described perhaps in a short story or a novel.

During the six or seven months we must spend here we must come to a definite decision about our future, and I must also devote that time to literary work of every sort.

Since I left for Bône in 1897 – how long ago that seems, alas! – I have neglected an art I love, namely drawing and painting. I plan to take them up again and while here, will try to take a few helpful lessons and acquire the odd notion about portraiture and genre painting in particular.

Our life, our *real* life will not take off again until after 20 February 1902.[47] What is that life to be? That is hard to tell, but as soon as Slimène is back, we will have to solve that question. If the Moscow business is settled by then in the form of a pension,[48] the best thing would be to go and create a peaceful haven somewhere in the

Tunisian Sahel – if it is not, the only feasible thing would be a career as an interpreter for a few years, somewhere in the South, it does not matter where – a few years of living in the desert, which would be wonderful, too.

The time has now come to face the fundamental question of what my life is all about . . . All the things that have happened so far have been but passing phases . . . ∪ *and Allah knows all that is hidden in the heavens and on earth.*

Money from the Villa Neuve estate remains held *in situ*. Augustin and his family are as destitute as is Isabelle and relations in the house are strained. To feed her habit, Isabelle resorts to smoking the leaves of the plane trees in the rue Tivoli. Isabelle does her utmost to earn some money for the family and even, despite her injured arm, manages to procure a couple of days' work as a porter at the Marseilles docks.

By 10 July, they have pawned their last saleable possessions, and Augustin the coat from his back.

Tuesday 23 July

Over here we have now reached the depths of poverty, which is all the more frightening as there is nothing I can do; had I been surrounded by people like myself, I could perhaps have managed on tiny sums to provide for tiny needs. But such is not the case, and they[49] have got appearances to keep up. For Slimène and myself, though, the end of our woes is near. I still need to lend a helping hand here, though, and that will not be easy. With what Slimène will earn and my way of keeping house, the two of us can scrape by in peace without giving up what little we need . . .

How will it all work out, though? There will be no way out if they do not accept to have their meals with us, for I will never have enough money to support two households. As soon as Zouïzou gets here, he and I will have to discuss it, unless the steps I will try to take *vis-à-vis* Reppmann[50] turn out to be successful. In that case I will let them have all of what Reppmann sends me, and they will then have at least the wherewithal to manage for a month, a month and a half, if Reppmann agrees to lend me 100 roubles, which is nearly 250 francs. That would save us all, for it would give the two of us a chance to set up our own little household, and buy the few things I need. Once I dress as a woman, I am bound to find a little odd job while waiting for something better.

With that in mind, I must make good use of the few days of solitude I have left and progress with my literary work as much as I can, write a few articles and copy them out, so that if I get any favourable replies from any quarter, I will have something to show and will not have to do any writing at the outset of our life together; that way I will not miss any opportunities that might turn up with newspapers and magazines after the summer.

There was a violent wind as I went to post a letter to Slimène, which may or may not reach him. I have very little hope. I went to Arenc on foot, and walked home via the Bar d'Afrique.

I will see tomorrow whether I can't earn a few pennies here and there writing letters in Arabic. I rather think that I am not going to lose heart. The one I fear for is Augustin. I just pray he will not think of doing what Volodia[51] did when he was down and out! As long as I am in the house, a collective suicide is out of the question. But after that?

∪ *May it please Allah* that we have seen the last of sombre dramas.

A thought to consider, which I found in *Notebook 1:*
Do as much good as you can today,
For tomorrow you may die.

(Inscription on the Calvaire de Tregastel, Trécor, Britanny) which is a paraphrase of the words of Epictetus:
Behave as if you were to die the very next moment.

Whatever the perils, agony and disillusions, one must remain steadfast the way cliffs resist the furious onslaught of the ocean's waves. One must at all cost do the right thing and preserve one's love of beauty.

Few people could survive my lot. I have now reached the depths of poverty, and may well be going hungry soon. Yet I can honestly say that I have never, not even for a moment, entertained the notion of doing what so many hundreds of thousands of women do.[52] There is not even a *temptation* that I feel I ought to fight. It is *out of the question,* period. I accuse no one, and will always feel more than tolerant of all human foibles, for they are all rooted in factors so dense and complex that only a few can analyse them.

Man's salvation, though, lies in faith. Not the dreary kind made up of empty formulas, but a living faith that confers strength.

To say ∪ *There is no god but God and Muhammad is his Prophet* is not enough, nor even to be convinced of it. It takes more than that to be a Muslim. Whoever considers themself to be a Muslim must devote themself body and soul to Islam for all time, to the point of martyrdom if need be; Islam must inhabit their soul, and govern every one of their acts and words. Otherwise, there is no point in mystical exercises of any sort.

God is Beauty. The word itself contains everything: Virtue, Truth, Honesty, Mercy . . . Inspired by such faith, a man is strong . . . His strength may even seem to be supernatural. He becomes what they call a *marabout*. As the knowledgeable and inspired Sheikh Ecchafi'r put it: 'Whatever you do, wherever you go, say: *'Bismillah al-Rahman al-Rahim.'* What he meant, though, was not merely to *say:* in the name of Allah, when one undertakes something, but actually to do things *only* in the name of God, to do only what is true and good.

Those are things I thought about for years, and after Béhima, I have come to understand them; no doubt the uninitiated, in their mindless craving for hollow phrases with which to mouth empty formulas, will shrug them off as mystical. If, as I hope and *think I can foresee,* it is written that I will complete the blessed cycle, it will be through Suffering, a path to which I sing a hymn of gratitude beforehand. One thing is certain, though, and that is that my soul has at last emerged from the gloom and limbo where it dwelt for so long.

Thursday 25 July, around 11 in the evening
I am finding it more and more difficult to stay here, especially in the absence of Rouh'. Neither Augustin nor Hélène is capable of loving me, nor will they ever be, for *they will never understand me.* Augustin has become deaf and blind to everything that fills me with delight,

he is insensitive to all of the sublime things I have understood at last.

I feel *alone* here, more so than anywhere else. The end of the month is in sight, though, and it cannot be long now before Zouïzou comes to put an end to these torments.

Received the two issues of *Les Nouvelles* from Algiers, dated July 19th and 20th, which carry the text of 'El Maghreb' and 'Printemps au désert'.[53] I feel comforted by that success, and it opens up some possibilities at least. It means that I must have patience and persevere. Above all, however, I must keep myself fiercely to myself and stop discussing my writing or ideas with people who do not *understand* them, and who do not *want* to understand.

There is no doubt that in spite of all appearances, it is destined that only I should be *saved morally* of all the people who lived the abnormal life of the Villa Neuve, an existence of which Augustin used to complain so much at the time and which he now seems intent on copying, to the most minute detail. I must at all costs adopt an order of silence, of impenetrability, to finish off this lamentable and horrible stay here.

I am not asking God for very much: simply that Slimène is returned to me, that we are married and that there is an end to this state of affairs over here. Augustin and his wife must find their own way out, and may they have enough to live on, as I have no way of helping people so diametrically opposed to me in every way.

Friday 26, 10 in the evening
To close this chronicle of the last six months of my life, which I began in sadness and uncertainty in hospital, I

have nothing but sorrowful and bleak things to report, although my spiritual progress remains steadfast. Of course, the reason for my depression of the last three or four days lies in my environment and its insoluble financial problems. At bottom my soul is serene.

The only thing I find really hard to bear is the delay in Slimène's return, and the enormous effort it costs me to be patient. Now more than ever am I in need of his beloved presence. My heart overflows with love and I feel irresistibly drawn towards him, for he is the last refuge I have left on earth.

Slimène is finally granted transferral to a regiment of Dragoons stationed in Marseilles, where he can serve his six remaining months in the army. On 17 October 1901, aged 29 and 24 respectively, 'Selimen Ehnni' and Isabelle Eberhardt are married in a civil ceremony. Having wed a naturalised Frenchman, which nationality is conferred through Slimène's father previously being 'honoured', Isabelle has also regained her right to live in any French territory, including Algeria.

Isabelle continues the narrative of this period of her life in Journal Four.

Saturday 29 October 1901, 4 p.m.
The terrors of three months ago are now mostly gone from our horizon. On the 17th of this month we officially became man and wife, never to be parted again. I am no longer forbidden to enter Algeria and in any event, my period of exile is almost over: we will be off for our beloved land across the sea in a month from now.

Isabelle adds the following entry three years later, just under seven months before her death.

Algiers, 8 April 1904, 9 p.m.
I have not recorded the thoughts I had in January 1902
. . . What does it matter? Three years later, in a different place of exile, in the midst of poverty just as wretched, of solitude just as hopeless, I see what ravages time has wrought in me . . .

Many other corners of the African continent still hold me in their spell. Soon, the solitary, woeful figure that I am will vanish from this earth, where I have always been a spectator, and *outsider* among men.

JOURNAL FOUR

Isabelle begins her fourth journal in July 1901, picking up from where Journal Three abruptly breaks off. She is in Marseilles after being expelled from North Africa, awaiting Slimène's transfer and their marriage.

'In the name of God, the all powerful, the merciful.'
THOUGHTS AND IMPRESSIONS

Begun in Marseilles, 27 July 1901. Finished at Bou Saada on 31 January 1903.

In memory of + the White Spirit.

Marseilles, 27 July 1901
After several days of anguish, I got up this morning feeling full of energy again, of patience, of hope and of an eagerness to get down to work.

If the torture of waiting for Slimène could only come to an end, if I knew the *exact date* of his arrival, this could be one of the best periods in my life from the spiritual point of view.

In the autumn there will probably be some funds, which means the end of many a problem, and above all of my feeling so powerless. Oh! To come into the money for that hapless Villa Neuve at long last and go and see Africa once again, who knows, perhaps even the unforgettable Souf at that! To be able to read again, write, draw and paint, enjoy the intellectual side of life and lay the groundwork for my literary career. Should

I be reasonable and, instead of going to Algeria, go to Paris with a certain number of articles for sale?

Slimène is suffering from bouts of tuberculosis. Isabelle, learning of his hospitalisation on 28 July, fears for his life. She receives a series of increasingly desperate letters from him.

1 August 1901, 11 o'clock in the morning
Had a letter from Slimène yesterday that has upset everything one more time. He has been in hospital since the 28th. How could I ignore those mysterious premonitions I have had all these years about the stages of my *via dolorosa*!

I am shaking from head to foot. Yet I must sit down and write, copy the text of *Amiria* and send it off to Brieux.[54]

The same day, half-past midnight
Slimène, Slimène! I do not think I have ever loved him so *purely* and so deeply as I do now, and if God wants to take him from me, let His will be done. After that I will undertake to go where there is fighting in the south-west, and seek out death, proclaiming ∪ *that there is no god but God and Muhammad is his Prophet.*[55] That is the only death worthy of me and of the man I love. Any attempt to make a new life for myself would be in vain, and criminal as well. It would be an *insult.*

Slimène wishes he had known my mother, but perhaps he will soon be with her. He can tell her our two hearts are *united for all time,* and how much they have suffered here below.

148

You who are up there, White Spirit, and you, Vava, no doubt you can both see the tears I am shedding in the silence of the night, and you can read deep down into my heart. You know that at his side I have purified my poor soul in suffering and persecution, that I have not surrendered and that my heart is pure! See for yourself, and as you have left us to fend for ourselves in this world so full of woe, call for God's mercy now on the two of us, mercy from that same God who put the White Spirit to rest among the faithful. Call for His punishment, too, on those who hound us with such venom.

Why did I not do as I had wanted and go off with Sidi Muhammad Taïeb, why did I not go and die with him at Timmimoun? Why did fate have to take that poor child away from the peaceful existence that was his, to make him share the doom that will be mine and saddle him with so much suffering and, perhaps, an early death?[56] Why should I not go off by myself? Does he regret having loved me, regret having suffered this much on my account?

Who will ever guess how infinitely bitter are these hours I am going through, these nights I spend in solitude? If any help comes my way, everything will be all right. No matter how ill he is, if I am there to nurse him, he is bound to get well, otherwise, bereft and needy as he is, his frail health will deteriorate, and that hereditary disease of his will have the upper hand . . .[57]

Tuesday 6, 11 o'clock in the morning
Mood *on the grey side*. Feel utterly fed up with present circumstances. Do not really care about a thing. Worn

out by bleak but vehement thoughts of the last few days. I have got the mental energy it takes to tackle what remains of the steps I have to take, but no enthusiasm.

Had a letter from Brieux: I realise that in the literary domain, I have a vast amount of work to do. Am determined *to do it, because I must.*

How strange: as I was writing the above, I felt a slight improvement in my outlook, no doubt because I think I might be able to do that short story for *L'Illustration.*

Thursday 8 August 1901, midnight
After reading Dostoyevsky as I do now every day, I suddenly feel a great deal of affection for this tiny room of mine. It looks just like a prison cell and bears no resemblance to the rest of the house.

A room that has been lived in for a long time will absorb some of its occupant's essence, so to speak, and thoughts.

Thursday 15 August 1901, 8.30 p.m.
I have been longing for the desert again these last few days, with an intensity so keen it almost hurts. Just to go as far as old Biskra's last *segniya*, where Slimène and I stopped that night *six long months ago*! Oh, to be free right now, the two of us, to be well-off and leave for *our* country! Will I ever set eyes on those magnificent wastes again?

On this wall are the drawings I did there, and the sight of *guemira* along the misty horizon fills me with nostalgia. Oh, to leave for distant parts, and start a new life again in the free and magnificent open air! Over here I suffocate between these four walls; I have never felt that I belong here.

To set off again, a vagabond, free and unencumbered as I used to be, however much it might mean in new suffering! To run as fast as my legs will carry me along the Quai de La Joliette – the only part of town I love *because it is the gate to Africa*, and board ship – a humble, unknown figure – and flee, flee at last *for good*!

Isabelle describes the unbearably strained atmosphere of Augustin and Hélène's house.

Friday 16 August, 11 in the morning
Oh, to turn my back on all this and go away forever, now I am far more of an outsider here than any other place. They do not respect the sacred things I hold so dear, for they are blind, a house of unseeing *bourgeois*, bourgeois right to their fingertips, and mired in the base obsessions of their brutish lives.

Yet they are *quite right* to push me to the limits of my endurance, for that way my heart lets go of them completely. These coarse and nasty scenes of theirs do not affect me any longer. I no longer care and only cling more passionately than ever to the beloved ideal that is my salvation and my *raison d'être*, and also to Slimène. From his letters I can tell he too has begun to think, a development that is bound to steer him along the same luminous course that I am pursuing.

All the pain I feel now is due to my being on tenterhooks while waiting for Slimène.

I must stop sacrificing all for the sake of people over here, and start thinking of a home of my *own*.

Reppmann and Brieux have no idea, especially Reppmann, that their largesse has not benefited me and that I did my begging for the sake of others, who simply took it all for granted![58]

Isabelle muses upon her sexuality, her lovers and her friendship with Dr Léon Taste, the doctor who attended her at the military hospital of El Oued. Something of a sensualist and radical, Taste found close rapport with Isabelle, and in some notes she commented that 'Doctor Taste soon became my intimate *friend*' and told her of 'his mistresses and his ideas . . . curious above all about sensual things and my past.'

Marseilles, Saturday 17 August 1901
I feel a deep uncertainty about Slimène's transfer. And then there is something else as well. To judge by his last letter, he seems to be thinking of the same thing as I am, namely the heady subject of physical love. The most delicious and unchaste dreams are visiting me these days. Of course I could not tell anyone about a secret like that, except Dr Taste, a confidant who used to be as brutal as he was sensitive.

There is no doubt about it, I do love Taste . . . physically the least attractive man I have ever known, at least where the senses are concerned. Not that I did not care for the man's eroticism, the way it would go from the rough and brutal to a form so subtle it would verge on the neurotic. I used to say things to him that no one else has ever heard me say . . . D.[59] is too down-to-earth and there is something about him that reeks of a tolerance too sweeping and too coarse.

Now that those people are all gone from my present life, I look back with amazement at a figure like Toulat,[60] and wonder if there, too, there is not some age-old atavism at work: how can the Arab way of life and what is more, the *Arab soul* have rubbed off the way it did on a Frenchman from Poitiers? Oh yes, Toulat is an Arab all right. He broods, and goes in for harsh and savage living in the desert; of all the French officers I ever knew, he is the only one who is not bored there. His very harshness and his violence are Arabic, in fact. There is also something savage about the way he loves, something un-French and un-modern, for love me he did without a doubt. His love was at its peak the day he wept such desperate tears when we came to Biskra. Love me he did, but he did not understand me and he was afraid of me. He thought the only thing to do was run.

All that seems so long ago! All the more so as I feel no more anger at the thought of any of *them*: the woman who used to think she loved those distant ghosts is now *dead*. The one who is alive today is so different, and she can no longer answer for past errors.

Certainly, sensual matters will always continue to interest me *intellectually*, and I wouldn't want to give up my studies in this area for anything in the world. But in reality, I now have a focus for my sexuality; for me, clearly the sexual domain is limited and, banal as it seems, to say, 'I'm not mine any more', it is quite to the point. In the sensual domain, Slimène reigns uniquely; is without contest. He alone attracts me, he alone inspires in me the necessary state of mind to leave the intellectual domain to descend – is it a descent? I very much doubt it – to the realm of amazing sexual realisations.

Our modern world is so distorted, falsified and off-course that in marriage the husband is hardly ever the sensual initiator. Stupid and revolting as it is, young girls are hitched to a husband for life, he is merely the custodian of her material virginity, and in the end he becomes a ridiculous figure. She is then expected to spend the rest of her life with him, usually in disgust, and suffer what is known as her 'marital duty', until the day that someone comes along to teach her, in the shadows of lies and deviousness, the existence of a whole universe of thrills, thoughts and sensations that will regenerate her from head to toe. That is where our marriage is so different from any other – and makes people so indignant: Slimène means two things to me – he is both friend and lover.

Just what did that strange, compelling man, Colonel de R.,[61] who held so many first-rate women under his spell, mean when he said: 'You are much sought after in Algeria' . . . ? Up to a point, that is something I know only too well, having found it out at my expense.

None of the men I have known, and that goes for the officers in particular, can understand what Slimène is doing in my life. Domercq had no choice but to accept it in the end. Taste *pretends* he does not understand, but he probably does. What does De R. think of it? I would certainly like to see that man again and get to know him better. There was nothing run-of-the-mill about the impression he gave me, and he cannot be an ordinary fellow.

So far I know nothing about Brieux's benevolent personality, except that he must be very kind . . . Is he unaffected like those brief letters of his, simple, open and straightforward, or is he the most complicated of them all?

Among the local figures of note, there is that nice man Mohammed ben Aïssa, who must have left for Algiers by now, and has a very kind heart.

Smaïne ben Amma – a man who is rotten to the core, finished, *warped* and just about spineless by now. His alcohol intake will either lead to *delirium tremens* or general paralysis. I could not find him more unpleasant, and there was no need for Zouïzou to put me on my guard against him. If I had to choose between that 'aristocrat' and the porter who likes his *kef*, I would definitely choose the latter.

Marseilles, Thursday 22 August 1901 noon
My ordeal is not yet over. Yet if I try to *reason* instead of giving in to instincts, there has actually been a change for the better in my plight: Zouïzou has left that horrible Batna, he is on his way and what is more, he is now in Bône, the city where Mother's grave is. May she make him feel at home, inspire him and take him under her posthumous protection for the rest of his life.

As for the situation over here, a highly intricate mechanism accounts for this intolerable state of affairs. + *No point in insisting.* Augustin is hardly to blame, in fact – except where his weakness is concerned – and that is not all his fault. He has made a fatal mistake in his marriage, and there is nothing anyone can do about it now.

My God, what a relief it would be if Exempliarsky were prepared to lend Augustin enough money to spare us any further expense that might be disastrous! We have so many debts and needs. Those 25 francs from the old lady would really come in handy. ∪ *May Allah lend a helping hand!* I must make a huge effort to get through this week without giving in to depression and put the time to good use – which is the hardest part.

The writer I like best right now is Dostoyevsky – perhaps because his novels remind me so much of the diffuse and hazy, troubled outlook that has bedevilled me for so long.

I reread my friend Eugène's[62] letters last night. My God, how he has changed in the six years that we have been friends! What a difference there is between his first rather green letters and his last ones, after his return from the heart of the desert, from places with names enough to make my imagination soar! What a pall has come over his soul. I have the feeling the romance he had in Algiers has a lot to do with it. The affair in question must have been serious and genuine to judge by his despondent letter, in which he wrote that he was off to the deep South, almost as if he were on the run.

I, too, have changed beyond measure since those days – even more so than he in fact. There is a yawning chasm between the child I was then and what I am now. No need to labour the point: compared with the way I was in Bône – only four years ago – there is such a difference I smile at the memory – sadly, it is true. No doubt my progress would have been far slower had it not been for the awful things I have suffered since Bône. The same thing would have been the case this year had it not been for *Béhima*. Everything I have seen and learned here has also had a profound effect on my character and will affect me for the rest of my life.

The only refuge, the only hope I have left in the way of a *human* relationship is Slimène, *and he alone*. All the others have vanished like so many barely visible ghosts, who may well have existed at one time, but only in my overheated imagination. He alone is *real*, he is no illusion and no sham.

Friday, 23 August 1901, 11 in the morning
Had an awful day yesterday, because of yet another pinprick from Augustin's wife.

Kept wandering through town from three to five in the afternoon, tottering on my feet, exhausted and worn out, looking for Smaïne. Did not find him. Went to Joliette, found my friend the porter. Borrowed 55 cents, sent cable to Zouïzou and bought some tobacco. Went home. Great fatigue, felt ill, pain all over my body.

Oh! to have to pretend! To feel there is an enemy at one's elbow, and not be able to leave! Why did I not go off today with Zouïzou's money? Because I do not want a break with Augustin, for I feel he is terribly unhappy. But the façade I put up fills me with revulsion and disgust.

On 24 August, Colonel de Rancougne gives Isabelle the good news that Slimène is permitted his transfer to a regiment in Marseilles.

Saturday, 24 August 1901, 10 o'clock in the evening
Allah has heard us at long last! The colonel came in person to tell me the transfer is official. Zouïzou will

definitely be here in three days' time, and we have the colonel's protection.

Oh, how enigmatic human destinies are! How unfathomable the paths on which God leads his creatures!

Monday, 26 August 11 o'clock in the morning
Having felt vaguely unwell these days, I had a curious fit yesterday . . . I lay down in the afternoon because I had a bad colic and pain in my lower back. By four o'clock I had developed a headache, that grew sharper by the minute, plus a high fever. I knew I was in a state of delirium, which wore me out.

They simply left me all alone in the house till 10 p.m., without any help whatsoever. When they did come home, they did not even bother to come in and see how I was. Thanks to Allah, though, I only have two more days to go in this horrible existence.

If I do not feel ill tonight, I ought to go and see the room at the hotel, for tomorrow I should go and look for the porter and for Smaïne.

Tuesday, 27 August 1901, noon
It has been a long time since I have felt as calm as I do today. The mistral is blowing hard, and it is a lovely autumn day. The air is pure and clear. It is cool outside, the sun is shining and *tomorrow I shall leave this house.*

To put it in a nutshell, I forgive them for everything, and let Him be the judge. I have done my human duty, and will keep doing it for the sake of my dead mother. There were times when I was in the wrong toward Her and Vava. Involuntarily so, of course, but I have got to make up for it by being straight and doing the right thing for its own sake and for Theirs.

Things have simmered down a bit, both in my outward circumstances and within my soul. There still are many questions to be settled, such as that of our marriage, which only raises a problem because we have no money. As we have the colonel's protection, I hope that all will be well on that score, too.

How many clouds are gone from our horizon! And most importantly, if God does not part us by death, the days of separation are now over *for good*.

Slimène arrives in Marseilles on 28 August. He and Isabelle rent a house in the centre of Marseilles: 67 rue Grignan.

29 August, in the evening
We have left Augustin's house. In the end, I pardon everything, and it is up to God to judge. I have done and will continue to do my human duty to the last.

At four o'clock, I went to Quai de la Joliette. Zouïzou arrived on the *Ville d'Oran* on 28 August 1901 at 8.30 in the morning, lovely clear weather, a strong wind . . .

The Villa Neuve is finally sold. However, all revenue goes straight into legal fees and Isabelle is left only with more debts.

1 October 1901, three o'clock in the afternoon, 67 rue Grignan
A month has gone by since I wrote those last lines. It is true that everything has changed. Zouïzou is with me here, and his health is not as bad as I had expected it to be. We are alone and in a *place of our own* – a delicious

feeling! We shall be married in a few days' time and the Villa has been sold.

Poor, dear Villa Neuve, I know I will never set foot in it again. Since finding out yesterday that *the house* was sold on 27 September, I have been haunted by memories of it, meaning the end, for good this time, of the story of my life there, my first life on earth.

Everything has been dispersed or is gone, all lies buried. In a few days' time even the old furniture, inanimate witness of our past, will be auctioned off and scattered. As for the two of us, the bond between us grows stronger every day, and once the next five months of exile are behind us, we will go as far down south as possible, and this time ∪ *please Allah, may it be forever.*

God has had mercy on me and heard my prayers: He has given me the ideal companion, the one so ardently desired, and without whom my life would always have been mournful and incoherent. For the moment we are having a hard and penniless time, but then again, + *only he who has suffered till the very end will be saved.* God knows what He has in mind for us. So one must be resigned and have courage in the face of adversity, in the firm conviction that life on earth is but a phase along the way to other, unknown destinies.

It has been a year already since that luminous, melancholy autumn in the Souf . . . The palm trees over there are shaking off their shroud of dust by now, and the sky is clear and limpid above the dunes. And we are here, in this dull and gloom-bound city!

The Nomad

Marseilles, 21 November 1901, 8 o'clock in the evening
For several days now, the two of us have been full of sadness, something I cannot quite define, and I am getting a premonition that we are about to leave; ∪ *God knows!*

Memories of the Souf, the buoyant love so deep in my heart for the country of my choice, it all makes for an obsession that is at once thrill and torment. I need only to hear the sound of bugles for a thousand feelings to start stirring in my heart.

Those are the same thoughts I used to have about the netherworld, when I would stand by the window in my room and daydream in the silence of the night, looking at the vast sky above the Jura's jagged, often snow-clad outline, and the black and heavy mass of great trees.

In the springtime there were always countless nightingales in the shadows of lilac bushes full of dew. A mysterious sadness would come over me as I listened to them sing. Particularly in childhood, my mind always found strange associations in ideas, memories and feelings.

It all comes back to me now, in the insecurity and sheer monotony of my present life.

For the first time since my beloved parents died, I am beginning to *exteriorise* a bit; I now have a duty to fulfil *outside myself.* That alone enhances the days I spend here, for they would otherwise lack meaning; the same goes for the five long months devoid of charm I have spent as an outcast in this city where I have no ties, where everything seems so alien and abhorrent.

Oh, how the *common herd* who pride themselves on their sophistication and their brains, abhor whoever does not toe their line and obey their asinine and arbitrary rules! How it rankles the common man to see anyone – and a woman at that – depart from the norm and be *herself!*

I am finding out these days that I have a talent I did not know I had for writing essays on such topics as history, that are not without a certain depth.

The worst thing that can happen to a human being is to become a sterile nihilist like Nicolas Stavrogin or a short-sighted, third-class intellectual like Augustin. The fact of the matter is that constant, genuine attention to things outside ourselves that *bring us no material gain* will mellow and uplift the soul and raise it above trivial, mundane concerns.

Now more than ever do I realise that I will never be content with a sedentary life, and that I will always be haunted by thoughts of sun-drenched *elsewhere*. The only place where I could accept to end my days would be El Oued.

26 November 1901, one o'clock in the morning
Feeling calm and sad today, longing to leave, to flee this room, this city and everybody in it.

It seems more and more likely that these will be the *last days* of our exile . . . God grant that this is so, since the Marseilles nightmare has lasted long enough!

What makes me very happy is that Ouïha is now getting closer to the arcane world of thoughts and feelings, so that I am no longer on my own there. It is clear that he is the companion I was always meant to have, and how unfathomable is the enigma that surrounds our lives on earth: we lived far apart from each other for ten, twenty, twenty-five years without either of us having the slightest inkling of the other's existence, yet we were both in search of the *one and only* partner, the one without whom there could be no happiness on earth.

The curious thing is that on 19 June 1900, in the grim and dirty room I had at Madame Pon's, I had the first hint of the sort of life that I might lead. I was writing a chapter of *Rakhil*, when, as if from nowhere, the notion of *going to Ouargla* struck me – that thought was the beginning of it all! If only we could predict, at each hour, the vital importance of certain actions, even words, which appear of no consequence at the time . . . There are no moments of our life that are without consequence or significance for the future. ∪ *Mektoub!* It is written.

To change the subject altogether: As I go over the history of Carthage with Ouïha, I am struck by the resemblance of callous Carthage of antiquity and present-day England: their greed, loathing and contempt for anything foreign, their boundless, intransigent egotism . . . Might those traits be characteristic of all great *maritime* powers? To broaden my vision further, I would need to make a serious study of history. Grocery bills and tailor's invoices are taking up the precious time that I would like to devote to thought!

Saturday 30 November 1901, three o'clock in the afternoon
It is freezing cold and all we have with which to keep warm is some wood given to us.

What will be the outcome of our present mess? If we manage to settle our worst debts and if my friend Eugène[63] sends me another hundred francs, we will of course leave for Bône on the spot and stay there for an indefinite length of time. When will we be able to head for Algiers? God only knows!

Yet despite all the trouble, the physical and emotional strain, there is one thing that delights me: Zouïzou's soul is constantly growing closer to mine. I have found the partner of my dreams at last. May he live as long as my life on earth lasts!

A thick, dark fog of conjecture and uncertainty is all around us. Yet there is one ray of hope, and that is that we may soon be on our way home to the country of our choice, probably to stay there for good.

I must make one sad return, quick and almost furtive, to Geneva.[64]

The army authorises Slimène's transferral to North Africa to serve his last month of duty. After seven months of exile, Isabelle and Slimène finally return to Algeria. Again destitute, they must at first stay with Slimène's family and attempt to scrape together some money.

Bône, Tuesday 21 January 1902
Sailed from Marseilles on 14 January at 5 p.m. on the *Duc de Bragance*. Reached Bône on the 15th at 8 o'clock in the evening.

Our dream of returning home from exile has come true at last; we are back on the soil where the sun is always young and shines eternally bright, the beloved land facing the great, blue, murmuring sea whose vast, empty stretches make one think of the Sahara in the evening, the Sahara which is now so much closer – a mere day's travel.

May this year mark the beginning of a turn in our lives, with the serenity we have yearned for and deserve as our reward!

Bône, Wednesday 29 January, 11 o'clock in the morning
Outdoor living and the simplicity of life down here are beginning to restore my strength. I had none left at the end of that long and painful period of exile in Marseilles. What is more, my brain is stirring, too, and I think I may do some writing here.

The very thought that the vast expanse of the Mediterranean now lies between us and that triple curse of an inferno in Marseilles where we were so miserable, that thought alone is all it takes to give me a feeling of *physical* well-being, of vast *relief.*

Twenty-one days from now, Zouïzou will also be free of his obligations to the army, so that he will have far more freedom and will no longer need to be wary of indiscretions. We will then have to manage by ourselves in this vast, magnificent universe that has its lures and disappointments.

The brief span of time I must spend on earth does not frighten me; the only thing that does is the thought that I might lose my partner and be left all by myself. As for my morale, *almost* total resignation and equanimity, which, as I have said before, all has a good deal to do with physical factors. I have no desire to have anything to do with the world at large and be a city-dweller once again: I am thrilled to be a hermit.

The two of us went by ourselves the other night to
meet Ali Bou Traïf on the Pont de la Casbah; we saw the
full moon rise over a tranquil sea. We paused at the turn
in the road that leads to the cemetery. The bridge looked
like the mystical one of the Slavic legend, the one that is
woven for nymphs out of moonbeams in the silence of
the night. All golden, it trembled slightly against the
waters' shifting background. A strip of grey cloud came
between moon and water, so that its shadow could be
seen there; and the shape of a low dune with two
promontories dividing the sea in two halves, one very
blue, vast and bright, the other a dull, misty grey melting
into the horizon. On the grey, there was a fishing boat
with a Latin sail. There was no reflection of it on the
waters' misty surface; it was not moving, but seemed
like a phantom vessel that vanished, evaporating slowly
into the distant fog.

**The pressure of living at close quarters with Slimène's
often hostile relatives has been hard on Isabelle. However,
despite such such circumstances and their poor financial
situation, she is feeling positive about her writing and
discusses her literary and journalistic aspirations.**

14 February 1902, three o'clock in the afternoon
A month has gone by since we left that inferno in
Marseilles and everything over here has already gone
awry because of the constant intrigues of these Moorish
women.

Here, as elsewhere, I notice Slimène's instability of
character and the damaging influence that his
surroundings seem to have on him. Will this change

some day? I don't know, and in any case, with such a character, the poverty to which we are now reduced is more than difficult. Far better to start another life of real destitution in Algiers – which would be less dreadful than in Marseilles – than to stay here, where hospitality takes the form of constant snubs and endless arguments.

My literary bent is stirring, and I shall try to make a name for myself in the Algerian press at least, while waiting for the opportunity to do the same in Paris. To do all this, I will have to have total peace and quiet for a while, almost to the point of seclusion. In Algiers, I shall have to find someone capable of teaching Slimène what he doesn't know, which is a major task.[65] That would take a lot of worries off my hands and leave me free to work. ∪ *Allah will see to it!*

I have less and less time for mundane problems and altercations. In fact, I look at everything and everyone with a much cooler eye. All I want to do is flee at any cost, for all the arguments and screaming is *physically* too much for me. If we could leave for the Karezas tomorrow or today, we would end our stay here with a few days of peace that might even turn out to be quite pleasant.

I shall go and say one more goodbye to the white grave, basking on its green hill in the exuberance of spring, and after that we will be on the road again, leading our lives according to the whims of fate.

After Slimène's official discharge from the army on 20 February, the couple move to Algiers. Isabelle resumes her solitary excursions and although now without a horse,

she travels by coach and mule, sleeping in the railway
stations and eating at Moorish cafés.

Left Algiers by a coach of the Messageries du Sud on 12
March 1902, at 6.15 in the morning. The weather was
bright and clear. Mental outlook – good, peaceful. The
journey up the slopes of the Sahel was long and
laborious. Birmandreis, Birkadem, Birtouta. Boufarik,
Beni-Mered. Reached Blida by half-past noon, went to
the café on the Place d'Armes. Had lunch at the station,
left again by the coach for Medeah. Sidi Medani; the
Gorges. Ruisseau des Singes; hotel; magnificent torrent;
narrow gorge. All along the road countless waterfalls
that vanish underground. At the 68th kilometre;
junction of the Oued Merdja on the left and the Oued
Nador on the right, which runs down the Djebel-Nador.
At the 70th kilometre: Camps des Chênes. Forester's
house and hamlet. Saw a soldier preparing his meal near
a well. Intersection of road No. 1 and the road to
Takitoun; memorial plaque for the Africa Army of 1855.
At the 74th, a farm. At the 75th, bridge over the river
Zebboudj. The Nador flows on the left, and the
Zebboudj runs into it near the bridge. After the 67th
kilometre the valley widens. Thickets of viburnum in
bloom and masses of ferns everywhere.

Reached Medeah by 8.30 p.m. Difficult climb over a
five-kilometre stretch. Visited Moorish café. Sent cable
to Ouïha. Spent some time sitting on a bench in the
square, and then in the café–restaurant at the station.

Set off again by coach for Boghari. Up at seven
o'clock. Left on horseback at eight. At first, a road

suitable for vehicles that passed by the civilian penitentiary. After that, Arab trails through a landscape of hills separated by deep ravines, covered with thickets and full of running streams. Stopover in a gorge with hot baths and a Moorish café.

Reached Beni-bou-Yacoub by half-past noon. Stayed there till two in the morning. Left by mule with two mounted servants. Road: high hills; gorges; deep ravines; countless *oueds*; sodden trails that had turned into torrents. Waded about all night long; lost my way several times.

At dawn, the valley looked dull and drab. Went on foot for a while to stretch my legs, which had gone numb.

Reached Hassen-ben-Ali by nine in the morning. Let the servants go. Got up at noon; went for a walk. A handful of European houses built of reddish clay, shabby-looking. High mountains for a horizon. Grey weather, strong wind, freezing temperature. At 3.30 p.m. went to the station and sent cable to Ouïha. Bought ticket. Icy drizzle. Walked along the single tracks.

Took train at five o'clock. Had to change trains at Blida, fell asleep on a bench. Was awakened by a labourer coming from Maison-Carrée. Reached Algiers by 9.35 in the evening on Friday 14 March.

∪ *Allah does not put the majority of fools on the right course!*

Isabelle meets Victor Barrucand, journalist and editor of *Les Nouvelles*, the paper that published her stories, 'El Maghreb' and 'Printemps au désert'.

30 March 1902
Present situation: no money. We rely on Si Muhammad
Sherif to come to our rescue and take care of us during
these last few days. During the day, I work.

Last Thursday went to see Barrucand at the Villa
Bellevue; had a pleasant impression.[66] A modern,
perceptive and subtle mind, although influenced by the
ideas of the century. Went to rue du Rempart Médée to
Mme ben Aben's workshop. Enjoyed my conversation
with intellectuals, something I had not experienced in
a long time.

A generous man will record the harm done to him in
pencil, the good in ink. *'Behave in this world as if you were
to live forever, and act as if you were to die tomorrow!'* to be
compared with Marcus Aurelius's thought on the subject
[Meditations].

**Slimène is studying for his interpreter's exams; Isabelle
assists him.**

1 April 1902, nine o'clock in the evening
We are still hard at work. We have so little time left – so
little! And so much studying to do to catch up that we
cannot stand it. It all takes a huge effort these days.
The trouble is, there are so many subjects. Well, ∪ *Allah
will help!* For the moment, I must continue to muster
courage enough for two, and when things are really
bad, cheer up Zouïzou and restore his optimism, for
without that we have no hope at all.

Barrucand said to me the other day: 'In life, there are
knots all along the threads of our lives. If we can manage
to get by those knots, we are temporarily in for a stretch

of smooth surface . . . until we reach the final knot, the Gordian one, which will be cut by Death.'

I think it is impossible for human minds to think of Death as a final, irrevocable end to life. As for myself, I have a *conviction* in the truth of *eternity*. Yet, ∪ *may Allah the Great forgive me*, if Death did really mean the end of everything, that would not be so bad. Does not, after all, three-quarters of all suffering lie in the memory we have of it, which is to say, in our *awareness* of it?

Victor Barrucand begins to help Isabelle financially, who is his protégée and intended journalistic collaborator. She is feeling more positive.

Algiers, 22 April 1902, 17 rue du Soudan
For once, we do not have too much work tonight. I have a moment to myself and after doing some translation for dear, kind Mme ben Aben, I have been reading Nadson.

Along the distant shores of the blue Rhône river, at the foot of the snowy Jura mountains, spring must be about to stir. The trees are covered in a mist of fragrant foliage, and the first rock plants are blooming at the Villa Neuve in the shadow of the pine tree and by the two graves in the Vernier cemetery.

Things are no different this spring from any other year, and Nature is doing what it always does . . . The difference is that I am no longer there to do my dreaming and my grieving . . . Vava, Mama and Volod have departed for the great Unknown! . . . Everything is gone, finished and destroyed.

The Nomad

Algiers, 4 May 1902, about ten o'clock in the evening
Went to see a magician today, who lives in a tiny place in a street in the upper town, reached by dark stairways in the rue du Diable. I have now found certain proof of the *reality* of this arcane and incomprehensible science of Magic. How vast are the perspectives such knowledge opens up for me, and also what a relief there is in the heavy blow dealt to my doubts!

I am in a calm and wistful mood these days. Algiers is clearly one of those cities that will fire my imagination, and certain parts of it in particular. I like the area we are living in, and our lodgings too, after the horrible hovel in the rue de la Marine.[67]

How can all those fools in 'social' and literary circles say there is nothing Arab about Algiers? There is, for instance, that lovely moment of the *maghreb* over the harbour and rooftops of the upper town. The place teems with merry Algerian women in their pink or green garments against the bluish-white of the helter-skelter pattern of the rooftops. I see them from the little *moucharabieh* window at Mme ben Aben's. And Algiers bay is, together with that of Bône, the most beautiful and marvellously intoxicating corner of the sea that I have ever seen.

Despite the dross France has introduced here by prostituted and prostituting 'civilisation', Algiers is still a graceful and good place.

I remember a time, though, when this luminous place was shrouded; the sight of a stretcher bearing a corpse underneath a thick grey cloth. A Kabyle girl named Zeheïra had leapt down a well in the Impasse Médée to escape a marriage she could not bear . . . the area where it happened still retains something of her shadow, and I prefer to avoid it.

The more I study the history of North Africa – very poorly and too fast – the more I see that I was right: the land of Africa devours and absorbs everything that is hostile to it. Perhaps it is the *predestined country* from which one day the spark will come to regenerate the world!

An old man once turned up at the French encampment after the 1830 landing at Sidi Ferruch. He had a pacific manner, and all he had to say was: 'There is no god but God and Muhammad is his Prophet!' With that he left and was never seen again. No one understood what he had meant by that. He had come to say that Islam and the mesmerising soil of Africa are one for all eternity!

8 June 1902, 11.30 at night
Life goes on, monotonous as ever, yet there is the hint of some *future direction* in the midst of all this dreadful emotional turmoil.

I am going through another slow period of gestation, which can be quite painful at times. I am beginning to understand the character of the two people, Barrucand and Mme ben Aben, who have helped us here, both of them good people and very tactful. Barrucand, a dilettante in matters of thought and in particular of sensations, and a moral nihilist, is, however, a man who is very positive, and *knows how to live*. Mme ben Aben is the second woman I have known after my mother who is good to the core, and enamoured with ideals. Yet in real life, how ignorant the two women are! *Even I*, as someone intimately convinced that *I do not know how to live*, even I know more than they do.

Augustin is now gone from my life. As far as I am concerned the brother I used to love so much is dead. That shadow of him in Marseilles who is married to 'Jenny the work-horse' does not exist for me, and I very rarely think of him.

Now that the torrid heat of summer has suddenly come again, now that Algiers lies in a glaring daze once more by day, the notion that I am back in Africa is slowly sinking in. Soon I will feel completely at home, especially if my plan to go to Bou Saada comes off . . . Oh, that journey! It will mean a brief return, not to the magnificent Sahara itself, but to a place nearby that has all the palm trees and sunshine one could want!

Remarks about Algiers

While the weather was cool, the shadows in the upper town's streets were grey and dark to the point of gloominess. Now that there is a sudden sharp contrast between light and dark, it all looks African again, or *Arab* in any event.

No, the true African landscape is not to be found in any of the large cities, certainly not in those of the Tell. African perspectives are hazy with a distant horizon. Vast space and emptiness, a blinding light, are what makes a landscape African! The architecture of Algiers boasts none of those traits. Its houses are all piled on top of one another and huddle fearfully at the bottom of culs-de-sac, in a city accustomed to raids and sieges. For lack of space, upper stories encroach upon the streets and straddle them.

Crowds do the Algiers street-life no good either. If there were shade and silence, those streets would have their charm. The mindless noise of motley crowds, where the only Arabs are those awful Kabyles in European garb, makes certain parts of town look like a place of ill repute where no one's life is safe.

The uninitiated European thinks those men in dirty *burnouses* over tattered European clothes, faded *chechiya* without a tassel, and many Moorish women are all part of the local colour. That is precisely what is so un-Arabic about Algiers, for it is contrary to Arab custom. The truth is that the maze of Old Algiers is medieval, Turkish, Moorish, or what have you, but not Arabic and certainly not African!

In the really Arab towns like the *ksours* of the south, the poignant and bewitching magic of Africa is quite tangible. They lie in the wide open space, the small, low, tumbledown houses, either very white or the same hue as their hazy environment, in all that light and bleakness.

The trouble with Algiers is its abject population. Any sort of contemplative street-life, of the calm and fertile, gratifying sort I love so much, is out of the question there.

The savage hatred I feel for crowds is getting worse, natural enemies that they are of imagination and of thought. They make it impossible for me to feel *alive* here, the way I do in other places. Oh, how evil civilisation is! Why was it ever brought over here?

Isabelle leaves Algiers for Bou Saada; the principal incentive for her journey is to seek a meeting with the *maraboute*, Lella Zeyneb.[68] She travels alone, taking whatever transport is available – coach, horse or mule, sleeping wherever she can find some shelter and relying on hospitality for food, which quite often amounts to little more than coffee.

The sirroco has arrived.

M'sila, 29 June 1902, two in the afternoon
I left Algiers yesterday, 28 June, at 7.50 in the morning. The weather looked ominous and cloudy . . . there were almost no stops, and the journey went by in a flash, as in a dream.

I am in a tiny hotel room, where I am waiting for supper. The heat is stifling. There has been a sirocco ever since we passed the Portes de Fer, and the countryside looks like a steam bath. The sky is misty in that incandescent way brought on by thunder.

The road from Bou Arreridj to M'sila goes through solitary places; some of them are parched, others marshy. Here and there runs a winding valley, lined with oleanders in bloom, its smell an acrid one of humidity.

From Madjez to M'sila, slept any way I could on top of a crate. Reached our destination by three in the morning. Went to the Moorish café, and to the market with Fredj. Had lunch inside the mosque, where it was cool and dark and there were relatively few flies. After that I came here for the siesta.

As always, it all feels like a dream, this journey, and sudden separation from Ouïha . . . poor Ouïha, who is without a penny and has got to cope with the ever worsening tedium of Algiers! If I could at least bring him some relief with this journey of mine!

I shall try to go back to sleep, so that I will not be worn out during the night.

Bou Saada, 1 July 1902
After a morning spent on clarifications with the El Hokkaïn, we spent the afternoon in a garden belonging to the *zawyia*.

With its picturesque setting, Bou Saada rather looks like old Biskra. M'sila is a town built of mud, and it is divided in two by a deep *oued* littered with stones. The greyish-brown houses have the dilapidated look of the *ksours*, an impression that is reinforced by the handful of dishevelled palm trees. The memory I have of M'sila is a gentle, poetic one.

It was the *maghreb* hour, and I went by myself to wait for Si Embarek[69] near the mosque by the *oued's* edge. The sun was setting in the sort of mist that always comes with the sirocco. On the other side of the *oued* stood the old part of town; its curiously shaped *marabout* shrines and its sombre gardens all gave it a decidedly Saharan air. Tahar Djadi's mare is an excellent horse and I could not resist the temptation to let her run a bit. I felt as if I were back in the best of the old days, when I had peace and freedom. We reached the *borj* of the *tolbas* after dark, a solitary edifice, square and sombre in its desert setting. Had a second supper outdoors by the wall. I then went off by myself into the night that enveloped the plains.

Had a bad night inside the courtyard, where I was devoured by fleas. When I saw the moon in its last quarter come up, pale and drenched in mist, I woke up the *talebs* and we left. We took a number of Arab shortcuts, via Saïda and Baniou. All we saw of Saïda in the early morning darkness were the black outlines of mud houses, without so much as a tree or garden; a grim sight indeed in the midst of that desert.

Farther on, while the *talebs* were saying the *fajr* prayer, I stretched out on the ground at the westernmost point. Si Ali, their *tolba*, then left us, riding astride the red mare whose graceful little bay foal trotted alongside.

We continued on our way by ourselves. Baniou, a *borj* built high up, and a handful of houses made of *toub*. An alleyway lined with poplar trees.

Had coffee thick with flies and a drink of muddy water, in the shadow of some tamarind trees growing in the sand.

In the *sebhka* before Baniou I felt so exhausted that I dismounted my grey mare and went barefoot for quite some time.

After Banou, we stopped at Bir-el-Hali: dilapidated houses made of *toub*, a well with good water. It was getting hotter and I continued my journey by mule.

Caught sight of Bou Saada among the bluish mountains, with its casbah set on top of a rock, and a handful of very low, small dunes that in the distance seemed white.

Arrival in Bou Saada. On one side of it are spacious gardens enclosed by mud walls. In the riverbed stand oleanders in full bloom. On the high ground on the other side stand the town's houses. It is a picturesque and hilly place intersected by lush ravines where, among the dark green of the fig trees and vineyards, the odd oleander strikes a bright pink note and the pomegranate trees in bloom, vivid scarlet ones.

The heat was torrid yesterday thanks to the sirocco, and culminated in a violent storm last night; it gave the place that beloved and familiar atmosphere. Bou Saada is surrounded by tall and arid, reddish-looking hills that block the horizon from view.

We dismounted under the arcade of the sheikh's house. Facing it lies a scrawny, walled-in French garden. To the left stands a munitions depot and an unkempt garden where frogs croak all night long. The population is obsequious toward the '*hakkam*', and a good deal more coarse and harsh than people in the Sahara.

Despite yesterday's heavy rainfall, the ground is parched. There are beautiful, slender-limbed camels of a Saharan breed that come to kneel down in front of the sheikh's house. I am alone, sitting on a mat beneath the arcade, with Dellaouï's little boy M'hammed, who will not leave me for a second.

This afternoon we will set off for El Hamel . . . When will I be coming home? When will I see Zouïzou? These are questions to which I do not know the answers. In any event, the journey alone has made it worth my while to come and discover this place which is, after all, part of my beloved South. In my present circumstances, the opportunity of this longish journey has been a golden one.

The women's costume here is unbecoming, in particular the huge, flat headgear. Unless the Southern women's costume is worn by graceful, tall, slim women, it is dreadful. The one worn in the Souf is prettier and has more style. I cannot say anything about the women's physique, for I have not seen any. The little girls are heavily tattooed and have pale and savage faces.

The Nomad

El Hamel, 2 July 1902, during the siesta hour
After the Turkish bath last night, we heard that Lella Zeyneb had returned to the *zawyia*, but the darkness of the night, the wind and rain all kept us from setting out. Slept beneath the arcade.

Woke up very early. Talked with Sidi Embarek until daybreak, and we set off together without any coffee, he by mule, I on a horse.

The village of El Hamel stands halfway up a slope, its highest point taken up by the fortress-like and green-shuttered *zawiya*.

Isabelle and Slimène move to Ténès. Having passed his exams, Slimène has been offered a job there as *khodja*, an interpreter. Ténès is a *commune mixte*, a politically volatile French–Muslim administration.

Isabelle is chain-smoking, and becoming increasingly addicted to alcohol and *kef*.

Ténès, 7 July 1902
My journey to Bou Saada was as rapid as a dream, and I came back feeling all the stronger for it and cured of the morbid indolence that had been plaguing me in Algiers . . . my soul, too, has begun to stir again.

A nomad I was even when I was very small and would stare at the road, that spellbinding white road headed straight for the unknown . . . and I shall stay a nomad all my life, in love with changing horizons, unexplored, far-away places, for any voyage, even to the most crowded and well-travelled countries, or the most familiar places, is an *exploration*.

The Nomad

Orléansville, 17 July 1902, 9.15 in the evening

Here I am again, back on the road, headed for Algiers. Luckily I will only be there for a few days for the *zawyia* and Mme ben Aben. After that I will go back to Ténès, where I shall have to stay.

I left Ténès at six in the morning, in lovely clear weather. I was feeling tired and sleepy. When I got to the Trois Palmiers, I found the local policeman and a good horse. Went to see the *caïd*, whose name is Ahmed. The house stands on top of a high hill where the view is very beautiful: the African landscape's arid slopes follow each other in a variety of colours into the distance. Set off again on horseback. Reached Orléansville by about six o'clock. It clearly is one of the prettiest cites in the interior, especially because of its setting. On its northern side it has a very high view of the Cheliff, and is surrounded by lush gardens.

I have been suffering from a severe bout of fever ever since I got here, and just then I more or less lost consciousness for a few moments . . . I am finding it difficult to write. I pray that I will not fall ill in Algiers, so far from my poor, beloved Zouïzou!

Ténès, 25 August, evening

I am sitting on an arid hill facing the valley and the chaotic mass of slopes and mountains drenched in mist. The tall mountains along the horizon stand out against the reddish-orange of the setting sun. All is peaceful in this Bedouin country, even though there may be the odd vague sound; the barking of dogs and the shouts of men who have come to lodge their complaints.

To the right, beyond the gorges, lies a hazy stretch of sea, to judge by the empty horizon. To the left, at the top of a pointed hill, a dense thicket of shrubs hides a handful of blackish stones that constitute a shrine, the grave of a *marabout*. Night is falling now and all sounds are dying down . . .

In Ténès, Isabelle and Slimène have again been thrust into the heart of political French Africa. Isabelle is suffering from the malicious gossip of her enemies; she in no way conforms to ideals of Western womanhood and continues her 'dangerous' association with the Arab community. She further damages her position by rejecting a demeaning sexual pass made by the French deputy mayor of the city.

Slimène's bouts of tuberculosis are worsening, and Isabelle is concerned about his strength.

Ténès, Thursday 18 September 1902, nine in the morning
The autumn has arrived. There has been a strong wind on quite a few occasions, and the sky is overcast with grey clouds. Now and then it also rains. Our life is as monotonous as always, which would not be so bad if it were not for the perennial money problems. Yet we do at least have the security of being able to satisfy our basic needs.

The problem with Ténès is that herd of neurotic, orgiastic, mean and futile females. Needless to say, here as elsewhere, mediocre people cannot abide me. In itself, all this mud-slinging means nothing to me, yet it does annoy me when it starts to get too close. There is, though, the precious resort of flight, of solitude on the open roads to the tribal villages, and the immutable peace found in horizons the colour of azure and pale gold.

I have visited many places here, Maïn, Baghdoura, Tarzout, Cape Kalax, the M'guen . . . I have been up and down the countryside, through peaceful Bedouin territory whose boundaries are still so vast.

As for my mental outlook, these last few days have been bleak, and strangely enough, as usually happens nowadays, Ouïha is feeling the same way I do. I am worried about his health. It may be, of course, that with regular treatment he will get better once and for all. If he was named *caïd* and if we went away from all the idiocy in Ténès, to some place in the mountains where the air is pure, with lots of rest and healthy living, he would certainly be happy.

As far as my literary activities go, these last few days have been a total loss. Today I am beginning to feel better, and this evening I will no doubt leave for the big annual feast at Sidi Merouan. My report on those festivities can give me the material for my next article for the ungrateful *Nouvelles*. The location and subject are just right for it. These last few days my health has been letting me down again. Is it the effect of my body on my mind, or vice versa?

Ténès is in the midst of the run-up to mayoral elections. Isabelle's closeness to M. Bouchet, rival to the corrupt and anti-Semite current mayor, means that she is again a political scapegoat. She keeps on the move between Ténès, Maïn and Algiers.

Maïn, 21 September 1902, ten o'clock in the evening
Once again I am the butt of the Algerian administration's boundless stupidity: the Commissioner has had a letter from Algiers. What will they think of next? The fact is that the little folk in Ténès have turned in a report.

I am here in Maïn, in a small, clean room. The only drawback is that outside my window the billy goat keeps bleating and leaping about with the female goats. Perhaps he will go to sleep at last . . .

I came here on my own, in clear, very windy weather. It takes a long time to reach Maïn. What is so strange and, on the surface at least, in total contradiction with the natives' character, is that the educated will confide in a woman like myself at the drop of a hat and talk to her the way they certainly would not to any man; witness the conversation I had with Si Elbedrani by the side of the road in the clear blue light just before dawn . . .

Maïn, 22 September, two o'clock in the afternoon
I am all alone, in this small room of mine; the heavy weariness of the last few days has *suddenly* evaporated and given way to a fruitful, salutary melancholia.

I have reread my earlier diaries. No doubt about it, my present life is sheer bliss compared to that of recent years, even the Geneva ones! And as for any comparison between now and the time I spent in Marseilles!

There is a silence here that feels eternal. I should like to come and live here (or some place like it) for months on end, to shield my eyes from the ugliness of European humanity, for I loathe it more and more.

The only person in Ténès I enjoy talking to is my friend Arnaud.[70] He, too, is despised by the band of pretentious philistines who think they amount to something because they wear tight trousers, a ridiculous hat or even a striped *kepi*. Whatever their unenlightened way of life, the lowliest of Bedouins are far superior to those idiotic Europeans making a nuisance of themselves. Where can one go to flee them, where can one go to live far from those arrogant, prying, evil beings who think it their privilege to level everything and fashion it in their own dreadful image?

I shall look into the possibility of settling in Palestine, once I come into the + *White Spirit's* money, which will no doubt be soon.

To escape from Europe, even transplanted Europe, into an Arab country, no doubt like the one I love, and live another life . . . Perhaps that will still happen! ∪ *Allah knows the things that are hidden and the measure of people's sincerity.*

Ténès, 26 September 1902, nine o'clock in the evening
The year has almost run its course, and so has this notebook. Where will we be a year from now, at the start of the rainy season when the countryside dons its pale shroud and takes its yearly rest, when asphodels bloom by winding roads? What ultimate direction will our destinies take?

It is cold and rainy. I worry about Ouïha's health in such bad weather.

It will not be long now before my journey to Bou Saada. Another visit to the South, its date palms, sandy wastes and grey horizons.

Isabelle discusses her position in support of the recent Muslim anti-French uprising. An attack was launched on the garrison at Marguerritte, the confrontation turning into a particularly bloody skirmish in which many were killed.

Algiers, Wednesday, 13 October 1902, five o'clock in the afternoon
I have been here for ten days now, far from those peaceful lodgings of mine and my sweet companion . . . I am feeling sad, in the way that always produces ideas. Curiously enough, I am beginning to get a better notion of this part of the country and savour its special splendour.

The great bay of Algiers is as smooth as a mirror. The opposite shore looks violet with its pink houses . . . Here on Mustapha's Hill all is peaceful.

The splendour of the moonlit night was unique last night. Its clear blue shimmer seemed to come from below, like dawn rising from the depths underneath the sea's transparent surface. Although sad, I am calm today. Right now, the moment of fruition is almost at hand. Fortunately, I am able to write.

I may have to go to France this winter to see about writing a piece in defence of the Marguerritte rebels. Oh! If I could only say everything I know, speak my mind and come out with the whole truth! What a good deed that would be! In due course it would have positive results and establish my reputation, too! Brieux was certainly right about that: I must start my career by coming out openly in defence of my Algerian Muslim Brethren.[71]

When will I go back there? I don't know. I must stay here for at least a week. After that I will have a great deal of work, for I will have to do a brochure, write an article a week for *La Dépêche,* and little by little collect enough short stories to make a book and have them ready for the day my name means something in Paris, after the Marguerritte trial. That means I will be taking a big step this winter towards peace and salvation, so that my Ouïha and I will feel more serene at last.

Oh, Mama! Ah, Vava! Look at your child, the only one, the only child to have followed you and to honour you, at least after your death. I am not forgetting you. I will always remember you. When things were at their worst, it was to you I turned.

Algiers, Thursday 30 October 1902
We had rain, wind and terrible storms for days on end while Ouïha was here. The sun has now come out again and with the return of spring-like weather, the countryside looks alive once more. In the mountains of the Chelha region it must almost be winter now. Its landscapes are more tortured and austere, its people live more simply, in silence and seclusion, far from the troubles we have here . . . I am beginning to long for all that, and above all for those long, solitary rides.

Ténès, Monday 1 December 1902, ten o'clock in the evening
The weather was beautifully clear on Friday morning when I set out for the boundary of Oran province. Until the Bou Zraya marketplace I had Lakhdar ben Ziou for a companion, a sombre and most unrewarding individual.

The road from Trois Palmiers to Fromentin passes by the foot of the Baghdoura heights. It is rutted and the poorly built bridges that cross the *oueds* are in a state of collapse, and before long all that is left of the road is a mere native trail. At one point the road goes by the foot of a hill that is overshadowed by a sharp cliff. The cliff's soil is a beautiful and warm reddish-brown. There is a brief glimpse of Fromentin in the distance in between two mountains, or rather two high hills. It is a recently built village full of eucalyptus trees, a place without character, like all those villages built on lands taken from those poor peasants, who now work there on the ruthless terms set by the French *khammesat*.[72] Those peasants do complain, but bear their lot with utmost patience. For how long will they, though?

The *caïd* of the Beni-Merzoug lives on a low slope below a hill called Mekabat al-Murabtine, named after the Murabtine clan, whose women are almost all prostitutes and about whom the strangest witchcraft stories are told. Two white *koubbas*: one, a very low, oblong building with a tall, egg-shaped cupola, on top of the hill, is new. The other stands at a lower altitude and is in ruins. The graves, heaps of stones or sticks, lie all around and down the slopes in the direction of the settlers' fields.

We could not find the *caïd*, so his son and I went back to Fromentin, where I was given a guide, an idiot by the name of Djellouli Bou Khaled. We started out and kept wandering aimlessly. He did not know his way around.

The next afternoon we went to see the Ouled-Belkassem clan, an hour and fifteen minutes away. They live in a *borj* and *mechta* surrounded by a thornbush hedge, in a magnificent site. The regal-looking Ouarsenis Mountains[73] towered above the entire expanse of the Shelif plain. To the left, Orléansville looked like an oasis full of black greenery. To the right, the first plains of the Oran region stretched out as far as the eye could see.

The reason for our going there was a sad one, and apart from the admirable panorama I saw, the memory I have of that lap of my journey is a grim one, for we went to see a little girl who had been burned alive in curious circumstances that will never be explained.

Everything is very peaceful in this remote part of the world, very far from any contact with Europeans, a place where it is still possible to find repose.

I have had an idea, and think it is a useful one. I was travelling slowly in the sunshine along the road between Baghdoura and Fromentin, munching on a deliciously crisp cake I had bought in the market and on some dried figs I had been given by my travelling companion: Write a novel, tell the unique story of a man – rather like myself – who is a Muslim and sows the seeds of virtue everywhere he goes. I must still find the plot, which must be simple and striking.

Today was the beginning of Ramadan, a time of year rife with strange emotions and, in my case, with wistful recollections. This is the third since the destinies of Ouïha and myself were joined . . . and we are happier now than we were then, sharing our lot and loving one another. The suffering of these three years has brought us closer than ten years' worth of prosperity could have done. For the moment our life is peaceful and free of any immediate worries. ∪ *'Praise to Allah for delivering us!'*

As controversial, easy political targets and hounded by their enemies, it is decided that Slimène and Isabelle should move from Ténès for good. Victor Barrucand offers lodgings at his house in Algiers, in return for Isabelle's assistance on his French/Arabic newspaper, *L'Akhbar/El Akhbar*.

Isabelle discusses the wrongs of colonialism, and her own battles with oppression.

11 December 7.15 in the evening
'It is one thing to know that somewhere in some distant place certain people are busy torturing others and subjecting them to every possible form of suffering and humiliation, and something else again to be present for three months during such torture and see such suffering and humiliation being inflicted every day.'
Resurrection, Leo Tolstoy

Algiers, 25 December 1902, half-past noon
The past and all its Christmas seasons are way behind me. My yearning for the past no longer extends beyond the Souf now.

The hardest thing to do, perhaps, is to *free oneself,* and what is more, to adopt a *lifestyle* that is free. I am increasingly resentful of mankind for its intolerance of unusual people, and for bending to slavery only to impose it on others. Where is that hermitage where I would be beyond imbecility and free of physical desires?

The same day, eleven o'clock in the evening
My discontent with people grows by leaps and bounds .
. . dissatisfaction with myself as well, for I have not
managed to find a suitable *modus vivendi*, and fear that
none is possible with my temperament.

There is only one thing that can help me get through
the years I have on earth, and that is writing. It has the
huge advantage of giving the will a free hand and letting
one project oneself without having to cope with the
world outside. That is its essential value, whatever else
it may yield in the way of a career or gain, especially as
I am more and more convinced that life as such is hostile
and a dead end. I trust that I can bring myself to be
content with living quietly as a writer.

As of now, I will probably go to Medeah and Bou
Saada once the five days of Ramadan are over.

Once again, my soul is caught in a period of
transition, undergoing changes and, no doubt, growing
darker still and more oppressed. If this foray of mine
into the world of darkness does not stop, what will be
its terrifying outcome?

Yet, I do believe there is a remedy, but in all heartfelt
humanity ∪ *it lies in the realm of the Islamic religion.* That is
where I shall find peace at last, and solace for my heart.
The impure and, so to speak, hybrid atmosphere I now
live in does me no good. My soul is withering and turns
inward for its distressing observations.

As agreed, I set off for the Dahra on the evening of
Thursday 11 December by the light of the Ramadan
moon. The night was clear and cool. There was total
silence over that desert town, as rider Muhammad and
I slipped through like shadows. That man is so much a

Bedouin and so close to nature that he is my favourite companion, for he is in total harmony with the landscape and the people . . . not to mention my own frame of mind. He is not aware of it, but he is as preoccupied as am I with the puzzle and enigma of the senses.

At Montenotte and Cavaignac we went to the Moorish cafés there. We crossed *oueds*, went up slopes and down ravines, past graveyards . . .

In a desert full of diss and doum, above a grim-looking shelf rather like those in the Sahara with shrubs perched high up on mounds, we dismounted to eat and get some rest. The place felt so unsafe that we started at the slightest noise. I spotted a vague, white silhouette against one of the shrubs down below. The horses snorted restlessly . . . who was it? The shadow vanished, and when we went by that spot, the horses were uneasy.

Our path led through a narrow valley intersected by many *oueds*. Jackals howled nearby. Farther down we came to the *mechta* of Kaddour-bel-Korchi, the *caïd* of the Talassa. The *caïd* was not there and we had to go farther still, until we found him in the *mechta* of a certain Abdel Kader ben Aïssa, a pleasant, hospitable man. We had our meal there and once the moon had set, we went off for Baach by paths riddled with holes and full of mud and rolling stones. At dawn, the *borj* of Baach, the most beautiful in the area, came into sight high up on a pointed hill, looking very similar to a *borj* in the Sahara.

Algiers, 29 December 1902, 2.30 in the morning
How curious and dreamlike is my impression – is it a pleasant one? I can't tell! – of life in Algiers, with all the weariness that goes with the end of Ramadan!

Ramadan! We spent its first few days over in Ténès, in the soothing climate of family life the way it is at that time of year. What a curious family we are, made up of people who have drifted together by accident, Slimène and I, Bel Hadj from Bou Saada, and Muhammad, who has one foot in the unforgettable Souf and another on those poetic slopes overlooking the blue bay and road to Mostaganem . . .

Isabelle is contemplative and ponders transience and her blood family's disintegration: the deaths of her mother, the man she calls her father, Vava, the suicide of her eldest brother Vladimir (Volodia), and the collapse of her relationship with her favourite brother, Augustin. She has been cut out of inheriting her mother's money by her half brother and sister, Nicholas and Nathalie, legitimate heirs to the de Moerder estate. In a final irony, all she is left is debt and lawyers' bills.

Algiers, 31 December 1902, midnight
Another year has slipped by . . . One year less to live . . . And I love life, out of sheer curiosity for nature and its mysteries.

Whatever became of my old dreams, those dreams of my youth, gazing at the snow-clad Jura mountaintops and great oak forests? Where are my beloved who have departed from this world?

Even when I was tiny, I used to think with terror of the time when those older than me would have to die. It seemed impossible they would! Five years have now gone by since Mama was laid to rest in a Muslim graveyard on Islamic soil. It will soon be four years ago that Vava was buried in Vernier over in the land of exile, next to Volodia whose death has never been explained. All around Mother's grave at Bône, Algerian winter flowers are now in bloom, and those two graves over there must be covered with snow.

And everything else is gone. That fateful, hapless house has passed into other hands. Augustin has vanished from the horizon of my life where he used to loom so large for so many years. Everything that once existed has now been demolished and destroyed for good. And for these past four years I have been roaming in anguish by myself, my only companion the man I found over in the pristine Souf, long may he stay at my side and bring solace, ∪ *please Allah.*

What does this next year hold in store for us? What new hopes and what new disillusions? Despite so many changes, it is good to have a loving heart to call one's own, and friendly arms in which to rest.

Algiers, Sunday 9 January 1903, midnight
It would be nice to die in Algiers, over there on Mustapha's hill, facing that sensuous yet melancholy panorama, facing the harmony of that vast bay with the jagged profile of the Kabyle mountains in the distance. It would be nice to die there, slowly, on a sunny autumn day, to be aware of dying while taking in the soft strains of music and inhaling fragrances as ethereal as our souls, which we would then breathe out together, in a slow, infinitely smooth and sensual act of renunciation, free of torment and regret.

Everything about my present life is temporary and uncertain. Everything is hazy, and the strange fact is that I no longer mind.

Who knows how long my stay in Algiers will last, who knows how it will end? Who knows where I will be tomorrow? Another journey southwards, in the direction of the desert, that blessed land where the sun is fiery and the palm trees' shadows blue upon the soil.

What I would like right now is to live over in Ténès, lead a quiet life there free of shackles, and keep going off on horseback in pursuit of my dream, from tribe to tribe.

After a period of brief and fragmented trips, Isabelle journeys to Bou Saada to visit the *maraboute* Lella Zeyneb. Her reward is a spiritual one.

Bou Saada, Wednesday 28 January 1903, half-past noon
Left Algiers at six o'clock on Monday 26th in clear weather. Reached Bou Saada at 7.30 in the evening, stayed at the Moorish bath. Never have I been so keenly aware here of the vaguely ominous weight that seems to hang over all the occupied territories; it is something one cannot put one's finger on, there are so many ambiguities and innuendoes, so many mysteries . . .

In spite of my fatigue, and lack of sleep and food, this has been a good journey. The Ziar are kind and simple people, and sang their saint's *medha* to the accompaniment of *gasba*, *zorna* and *bendar*, each in turn, while the train wended its way in the sunshine I was so happy to have found again.

Chellal is a cheerless village built of mud; a handful of wretched cottages set in a hollow full of water. An acrid smell of iodine and saltpetre hangs in the air. The native population is made up of Ouled-Madhi and of

Hachem, who are not very congenial. The *maghreb* was superb, with the mountains standing out in bluish-black against the red-gold of the sky.

I visited the Arab Bureau this morning, and by about one o'clock I went for a stroll in the Arab part of town, and in the *oued*, where Arab washerwomen stood out in blue and red dots of an incredibly warm intensity.

Tomorrow I will go to El Hamel. Once I have had some rest tomorrow night, I will do a better job of writing down my observations. The physical fatigue and lack of food I have suffered until tonight have worn me out. The ride to El Hamel will be good training for the long journey to Sahari and Boghar.

It looks as if I am no longer being persecuted. They tell me there had been no advance word of my arrival, yet they have been most pleasant, even the commanding officer . . . how shadowy and mysterious these people are!

El Hamel, Thursday 29 January 1903, about four in the afternoon
There is a heavy silence all around and the only sound to break it is the occasional noise coming from the village or the *zawyia*, the distant sound of dogs barking and the raucous growls of camels.

El Hamel! How appropriate that name is for this corner of old Islam, so lost in these barren mountains and so veiled in unfathomable mystery.

The same evening, about ten o'clock
I am sitting on my bed, near the fireplace in the vaulted main room. The fire and my bed right on the floor

make the room look so much more cheerful and cosy than it did earlier in the day.

The 'hotel', a large square edifice, boasts a deep and desolate-looking inner courtyard full of bricks and stones. It leads to the upper floor which is divided into two rooms, a small and a large one, both of them with semicircular vaults, like well-to-do houses in the Souf. One of the windows looks out over the cemeteries in a south-westerly direction, the three others give out on to the east. There are three French beds, an oval table, chairs, all of it set on very thick rugs. With a few more authentically Arab touches, the room would look truly grand. I wish I could arrange it myself and do it justice. On the western side stand the tall buildings made of *toub* where the *maraboute* lives. To the north is the new mosque with its great, round cupola surrounded by smaller ones, and inside it stands the tomb of Sidi Muhammad Belkassem.

I am going to lie down and rest, for tomorrow I must rise early to go and see the *maraboute*. No doubt I will return to Bou Saada tomorrow afternoon, and will try to be there by the *maghreb*. After that I will have a week for a good look, and that is a time I must not waste.

Bou Saada, Saturday 31 January, one o'clock in the afternoon
We arrived here from El Hamel yesterday at three in the afternoon.

Every time I see Lella Zeyneb I feel rejuvenated, happy for no tangible reason and reassured. I saw her twice yesterday in the course of the morning. She was very good and very kind to me, and was happy to see me again.

Visited the tomb of Sidi Muhammad Belkassem, small and simple in that large mosque, and which will be very beautiful by the time it is finished. I then went on to pray on the hillside facing the grave of El Hamel's pilgrim founders.

I did some galloping along the road, together with Si bel Abbès, under the paternal gaze of Si Ahmed Mokrani. Some women from the brothel were on their way back from El Hamel. Painted and bedecked, they were rather pretty, and came to have a cigarette with us. Did *fantasias* in their honour all along the way. Laughed a lot . . .

The legend of El Hamel's pilgrims appeals to my imagination. It must be one of Algeria's most biblical stories . . .

I began this diary over in that hated land of exile, during one of the blackest and most painfully uncertain periods in my life, a time fraught with suffering of every sort. Today it is coming to an end.

Everything is radically different now, myself included.

For a year now I have been on the blessed soil of Africa, which I never want to leave again. In spite of my poverty, I have still been able to travel and explore unknown regions of my adoptive country. My Ouïha is alive and we are relatively happy materially.

This diary, begun a year and a half ago in horrible Marseilles, comes to an end today, while the weather is grey and transparent, soft and almost dream-like here in Bou Saada, another Southern spot I used to yearn for over there!

I am getting used to this tiny room of mine at the Moorish bath; it is so much like me and the way I live. I will be staying here for a few more days before setting off on my journey to Boghar, through areas I have never seen; living in this poorly whitewashed rectangle, a tiny window giving out on the mountains and the street, two mats on the floor, a line on which to hang my laundry, and the small torn mattress I am sitting on as I write. In one corner lie straw baskets; in the opposite one is the fireplace; my papers lie scattered about . . . And that is all. For me that will do.

There is no more than a vague echo in these pages of all that has happened these last eighteen months; I have filled them at random, whenever I have felt the need to *articulate* . . . For the uninitiated reader, these pages would hardly make much sense. For myself they are a vestige of my earlier cult of the past. The day may come, perhaps, when I will no longer record the odd thought and impression in order to make them last a while. For the moment, I sometimes find great solace in rereading these words about days gone by.

I shall start another diary. What shall I record there, and where shall I be, the day in the distant future when I close it, the way I am closing this one today?

∪ *'Allah knows what is hidden and the measure of people's sincerity!'*

Isabelle's diaries end here. In the year and nine months following this last entry, she continued working, writing of her impressions of the Souf, and in her solitary travels traversing the desert.

In October 1904, suffering from bouts of malaria and very likely infected with syphilis, Isabelle was hospitalised at the hillside garrison of Aïn Sefra. After prematurely discharging herself, she wrote to Slimène, requesting he join her.

On 21 October, the day after Slimène's arrival, the town of Aïn Sefra was struck by a freak flood; torrential mountain waters rushed down the *oued*, engulfing houses and claiming the inhabitants. Slimène escaped. Isabelle Eberhardt was killed, aged just twenty-seven. Her body was discovered crushed by rubble. She was dressed as Si Mahmoud, her arms clasped above her head in a final gesture of defence.

NOTES

∪ Arabic + Russian

1. The cemetery in Annaba where Isabelle's mother, Mme de Moerder, is buried. Bône was the French colonial moniker for Annaba, which is now reverted to the original Arabic, along with most French street names of Algerian towns. As a testament to the regard in which Isabelle was held by Arab North Africa, an Algiers street bearing her name remains unchanged.

2. Alexander Trophimowsky, Isabelle's tutor and probably her father. An ex-priest of the Russian Orthodox Church; an anarchist and Bakuninist; an erudite scholar and linguist, fluent in French, Italian, German, Hebrew and Arabic as well as his mother-tongue, Russian. His Armenian background ensured his fascination with Islam, a preoccupation that was passed on to Isabelle. Trophimowsky believed in sexual equality, and in charge of Isabelle's education, he kept her hair in a utilitarian crop and dressed her as a boy.

3. Isabelle's favourite brother, with whom she felt the most affinity and experienced an intense childhood relationship. Idolising him in his rebellious youth, she fantasised about their forging a life together in North Africa, the Maghreb of their children's imagination. The 'wedge' of their separation is in probable reference to Augustin's recent marriage and embracement of a 'respectable' lifestyle. Isabelle did not get on well with his new bride Hélène, who came to view her sister-in-law Isabelle as an embarrassment to her and her husband.

4. Eugène Letord, a French Lieutenant based initially in Algeria, with whom she began correspondence in 1896, having responded to his Personals advert in the paper. He was the first to suggest to Isabelle that she move to North Africa and was a good friend to her throughout her life. For a brief period on their meeting in Batna in 1899, Letord and Isabelle were probably lovers. Isabelle described Letord as the only European man that she had ever found sexually attractive.

5. One of the Berber tribes of North Africa.

6. Isabelle is perhaps thinking of vengeance for the social execration that she and her family have suffered.

7. Ahmed Rachid, whom Isabelle calls 'Archivir', a young diplomat of Muslim Armenian extraction, a secretary in the Ottoman Embassy in Paris. An intelligent and intense individual, Isabelle and he met some time after the death of her mother in 1897 and before that of

Trophimowsky in 1899, and Rachid rapidly fell in love with her. His next posting was suspected to be to North Africa, and they began to plan to live there together, married in a Muslim ceremony. The posting in fact turned out to be for Holland. Perhaps a combination of this disappointment and Rachid's request that she grow her hair for him implicitly curtailing her independence, pushed Isabelle, in 1898, to end the relationship, although he would feature in her contemplations for some years to come.

8. *Mektoub*, Arabic meaning, 'That which is written.' Islam's foundations of destiny, fate, an individual's path in life and God's intention.

9. The adjacent graves of Isabelle's brother, Vladimir, and Trophimowsky at the hillside cemetery of Vernier in Switzerland.

10. The Muslim cemetery in Bône where Mme de Moerder, Isabelle's mother, is buried.

11. Ahmed Rachid.

12. Isabelle's novel, *Rakhil*. The story focuses upon a love affair between Rakhil, a Jewish prostitute, and a well-to-do, Paris-educated Muslim, Mahmoud. The narrative articulates a recurring concern of Isabelle's; the pollution of an old society and culture by transient and vapid, sophisticated modern notions. Isabelle was never to finish writing *Rakhil*, and the incomplete manuscript found after her death was rendered almost illegible from the flood that killed her.

13. Isabelle reads and rereads her diaries, often adding comments later in the margins of the pages. Next to this she has written: 'In memory of that fateful date, 16 June 1900. That is how my fate was sealed, either by some unconscious mechanism or by pure inspiration. From the recesses of my soul came all of a sudden a picture of the road to be followed, the very road that was to lead me to the Bir R'Arby garden and to Slimène, to the *khouans*, Béhima, and salvation. Marseilles, 23 July 1901.'

14. Only a fragment of *La Voie* has survived.

15. Isabelle later wrote in the margin: 'A few days later, the *Mektoub* saw to it that my lot was tied to Slimène's forever.'

16. Isabelle wrote in the margin in 1901: 'My Faith comes first, my Art comes next, and that is right, for those are the productive forces that embrace the universe.'

17. Isabelle wrote in the margin: 'The only thing that makes sense is the written word.'

18. Eugène Letord.

19. Isabelle's first recorded experience of *kef* (hashish) smoking, is in 1899, although she may well have tried it earlier (along with other narcotics such as opium) with Augustin in Geneva. Already an inveterate cigarette-smoker, she was to become heavily addicted to both *kef* and alcohol.
20. French colonial administration in North Africa.
21. Isabelle wrote in the margin alongside this entry, presumably a year later: 'A year's span! A year has gone by, and my life is linked to his forever!'
22. It has been suggested that, although genuinely impressed by her devotion, El Hussein suspected that Isabelle was affiliated with the French authorities and believed she could be useful to him.
23. Isabelle wrote later in the margin, dated 22 December 1900: 'A few days later, the house where we had that siesta was ravaged by typhus, which killed five people.'
24. The year of Mme de Moerder's death in Algeria. Isabelle had accompanied her mother on this last journey to the South.
25. Pierre Loti's first book, published in 1879. With its charged depictions of Turkey and the 'Orient', the novel exerted an imaginative pull upon Isabelle from her teenage years.
26. Si Hachemi ben Brahim, whom Isabelle refers to as Si Lachmi.
27. Isabelle's lasting attraction to El Hachemi/Si Lachmi is powerful. A controversial figure with a reputation for underhandedness and scandal, Isabelle is later accused of being his mistress, although the truth of this claim is uncertain.
28. Slimène.
29. Isabelle means Slimène here, not Augustin.
30. The village of Béhima, location of Isabelle's attempted assassination.
31. Slimène.
32. The end-date of Slimène's term in the army.
33. Slimène.
34. Isabelle and Slimène wished to marry. Despite Isabelle's letters, Augustin had not corresponded with Isabelle since she left France nearly a year previously. Slimène wrote to him, describing Isabelle's sadness at his silence. Finally, he replied making a gesture of reconciliation and giving his blessing to their union, a relationship of which he had openly disapproved.
35. General Pujat, commander of Touggourt. Despite Isabelle's suspicions that he ordered her assassination in order to remove a

political menace, Pujat in fact regarded her benignly, as a 'crank rather than as anyone dangerous' and merely ordered her 'strict but discreet surveillance'. The accusation that the French Military had a hand in the assassination is, however, not without grounding.

36. A rival religious brotherhood to the Qadrya, the confraternity to which Isabelle belonged. The Tidjanya were thought to be associated with the French.

37. Two years earlier, on first arriving in Batna and later in Biskra, Isabelle had thrown money from the window of her lodgings in a gesture of anti-materialism and as an emblem of her new-found freedom. Such extravagant gestures were noted by *colons* and locals alike.

38. The forthcoming trial of her assassin, Abdallah Mohammed ben Lakhdar, at the court in Constantine.

39. Hélène, Augustin's child, who bore a striking resemblance to Isabelle.

40. A moot point: was Abdallah acting on behalf of the Tidjanya in a violent message to the Qadrya; was he hired by the French to remove a 'nuisance' to colonial peace; or was he even contracted by El Hachemi/Si Lachmi to get rid of a mistress who had served her purpose and was less close to the French authorities than he'd hoped?

41. An exaggeration: in time Isabelle recovered full use of her arm.

42. The Tidjanya's hatred stemmed from their rivalry: as the oldest Sufi clan, the Qadrya were party to a mystical tradition that the Tidjanya were not.

43. Isabelle travelled extensively in 1899 and, disguised as Si Mahmoud Essadi, her adventures were sexual as well as cultural.

44. El Hachemi/Si Lachmi.

45. Isabelle is thinking of her becoming a *maraboute*. However, it is highly unlikely that Isabelle, a European woman, promiscuous and cross-dressing, would have been permitted *maraboute* status, a predominantly inherited religious and political standing.

46. Abdallah's defence lawyer.

47. The end-date of Slimène's term in the army.

48. Mme de Moerder's money in Russia, left to her by her first husband, the General, on the proviso that she apply for it at regular intervals in person.

49. Augustin and Hélène.

50. An old friend of the family and Isabelle's editor and journalist contact in Russia.

51. Isabelle refers to her brother Vladimir's suicide in 1898. He gassed himself in the Villa Neuve's domestic oven. In 1914, only ten years after Isabelle's death, Augustin was also to end his life.
52. Isabelle means prostitution.
53. Isabelle's short stories 'El Maghreb' and 'Printemps au désert' were published in the Algiers-based *Les Nouvelles*, 19 and 20 July 1901.
54. Isabelle's friend, the playwright and editor, Eugène Brieux, who assisted Isabelle with her journalism.
55. There was fighting on the Moroccan border at this time.
56. Isabelle means Slimène.
57. Isabelle's fears are thankfully unrealised; Slimène eventually recovers from this latest bout of tuberculosis.
58. Both Reppmann and Brieux lent Isabelle money, most of which is spent by Augustin and Hélène.
59. Domercq, one of Isabelle's past lovers.
60. A French officer, one of Isabelle's past lovers.
61. Colonel de Rancougne, a friend who gave Isabelle and Slimène much official assistance, obtaining Slimène's permutation to Marseilles and the approval for their marriage.
62. Eugène Letord.
63. Eugène Brieux.
64. Isabelle travelled to Geneva for ten days on 21 December, visiting her lawyer to try to put her affairs in order before leaving for North Africa.
65. Isabelle refers to the tutoring needed in preparation for Slimène's interpreter's exams. She had begun to have doubts about Slimène's intellectual ability and application to work.
66. With a strong foundation of mutual respect, Isabelle and Victor Barrucand's friendship developed over the years. Barrucand continued to help Isabelle throughout her life, finding her employment and defending her interests, as well as championing her work after her death and editing her writing – though with rather too free a hand for changes – for its posthumous publication.
67. On reaching Algiers on 14 March, Isabelle and Slimène rented very poor dwellings in rue de la Marine, before moving to slightly more salubrious accommodation in rue du Soudan.
68. Nearly fifty, and without brothers, Lella Zeyneb inherited her *maraboute* status from her father.
69. A guide and member of the Qadrya.

70. Robert Arnaud, better known by his pen-name of Robert Randau, the French Orientalist, writer and local magistrate, with whom Isabelle became firm friends. In his recollections of Isabelle, published in 1945 as *Notes et Souvenirs*, he remarks upon her 'extraordinary shining black eyes'. Although naturally piercing, the gleam of her eyes was probably augmented by her admitted drug and heavy *kef*-smoking habit.

71. Although vocal in her support of the colonised North Africans, Isabelle never completed and published an article specifically defending either the rebels at the Marguerritte trials, or condemning the subjugation of North Africans in general.

72. An exploitative agricultural policy in which the North African peasant-farmer received only a fifth of the produce of the land upon which he had worked.

73. L'Oeil du monde, perhaps the most stunning peak of the Algerian Atlas Mountains.

GLOSSARY

asr	afternoon; the afternoon prayer
bach-adel	notary
bach-hamar	leader of donkey or camel drivers
bendar	drum
borj	outpost
burnous	traditional North African hooded cape, worn by men
caïd	religious notable
chechiya	headdress
chih	aromatic plant
chira	marijuana variety
colon	colonist
deïra	head of locality
diss	a herb
djerid	palm leaves
doum	a herb
fajr	dawn; the morning prayer
fatiha	opening verse of the Koran
fellah	peasant
gasba	flute
gourbi	roughly-built hut
guerba	waterskin
hakkam	French colonial leader of a locality
hamel	porter
icha	evening; the evening prayer
imam	leader of prayers in a mosque
Kabyle	Berber tribe of North Africa
kachébia	Arab cloak
kepi	North African cap
khodja	interpreter
khouan	initiate into a religious brotherhood, such as the Qadrya
kef	hashish, a variety of marijuana, literally translating as 'high'
koubba	dome
ksar/ksours	county/ies
maghreb	literally translating as 'where the sun sets', used to refer to the countries of NW Africa; twilight

207

	(the time of day of the sun's setting); the *maghreb* prayer
marabout/e	religious and political role
mechta	area surrounding the *gourbi* shanty towns
medha	religious ceremony praising God
Mektoub	'That which is written', a premise of Islam
mihrab	altar
mokkadem	local sheikh
moucharabieh	wooden shutters
naïb	delegate of a sheikh
nefsaoua des bendar	dervishes with drums
oued	valley, ravine, stream or river, often parched dry
oumara	vessel, often for water
Qadrya	religious brotherhood
roumi	literally 'Roman', used to refer to Christians and Westerners
sebhka	salt flat/lake
segniyas	a place to keep arms
sherif	descendent of the Prophet Muhammad; a figure of high regard
shott	salt flat/lake
taleb	student of the Koran
thuja	fragrant flowering plant
Tidjanya	religious brotherhood
tolba	teacher of students of the Koran
toub	mud
toubib	doctor
wakil	keeper of the mosque
zawyia	Muslim monastary, home of the *marabouts*, haven for rest and sanctuary for those persecuted and a school of theology and la
zériba	a stable or sty
ziara	pilgrimage
zorna	flutes